Consumer Health Information Services and Programs

Consumer Health Information Services and Programs

Best Practices

Edited by M. Sandra Wood

ROWMAN & LITTLEFIELD
Lanham • Boulder • New York • London

Published by Rowman & Littlefield
A wholly owned subsidiary of The Rowman & Littlefield Publishing Group, Inc.
4501 Forbes Boulevard, Suite 200, Lanham, Maryland 20706
www.rowman.com

Unit A, Whitacre Mews, 26-34 Stannary Street, London SE11 4AB

British Library Cataloguing in Publication Information Available

Library of Congress Cataloging-in-Publication Data

Names: Wood, M. Sandra, editor.
Title: Consumer health information services and programs : best practices / edited by M. Sandra Wood.
Description: Lanham : Rowman & Littlefield, [2016] | Series: Best practices in library services | Includes bibliographical references and index. | Description based on print version record and CIP data provided by publisher; resource not viewed.
Identifiers: LCCN 2015044028 (print) | LCCN 2015042629 (ebook) | ISBN 9781442262744 (electronic) | ISBN 9781442262720 (cloth : alk. paper) | ISBN 9781442262737 (pbk. : alk. paper)
Subjects: LCSH: Medicine—Information services. | Health—Information services. | Public health libraries. | Health education.
Classification: LCC R118.2 (print) | LCC R118.2 .C65 2016 (ebook) | DDC 362.1—dc23
LC record available at http://lccn.loc.gov/2015044028

♾️™ The paper used in this publication meets the minimum requirements of American National Standard for Information Sciences—Permanence of Paper for Printed Library Materials, ANSI/NISO Z39.48-1992.

Printed in the United States of America

Contents

List of Figures and Tables   vii

Preface   ix

Acknowledgments   xv

1   A Most ResourceFULL Consumer Health Information Center   1
Cara Marcus

2   The University of Tennessee Medical Center's Preston
Medical Library and Health Information Center Story   19
Sandy Oelschlegel, Martha Earl, and Kelsey Leonard

3   Health InfoNet of Alabama   35
Kay Hogan Smith

4   Consumer Health Information Service in the Public Library   51
Barbara M. Bibel

5   Rewards and Challenges of Children's Health Education: An
Ongoing Community Partnership to Reach Local Preschoolers   67
Deidra Woodson and Donna F. Timm

6   Collaborative Outreach between a Hospital Library and a
Public Library   87
Margot Malachowski, Anne Gancarz, and Ellen Brassil

7 Consumer Health and the Department of Veterans Affairs
Library Network   103
*Priscilla L. Stephenson, Teresa R. Coady, Diane K. Kromke,
Laurie A. Barnett, and Cornelia E. Camerer*

8 The Learning Center: A Cancer Consumer Health Library
at MD Anderson Cancer Center   119
Elizabeth Brackeen

9 The Big Health Library Umbrella: Our Mandate to Provide
Information for All Literacy Abilities   133
Jackie Davis

Index   151

About the Editor and the Contributors   157

List of Figures and Tables

FIGURES

1.1 A BookTalk in the Patient/Family Resource Center   4

1.2 P/FRC volunteers are ready to help   8

1.3 Healthy Sleep Open House   17

2.1 UT Medical Center Health Information Center floor plan   27

2.2 View of the UT Medical Center Health Information Center from lobby   27

2.3 Patient-centered space and book collection at UT Medical Center Health Information Center   28

3.1 Health InfoNet of Jefferson County website, December 2001   40

3.2 NICHSR-funded promotional billboard, located in Birmingham, Alabama, 2009   43

5.1 Children boo at a cupcake during the Grocery Bag game   72

5.2 Deidra Woodson poses with the Healthy Garden game   73

5.3　With the help of adults, children create their own sun hats　　75

5.4　Portable healthelinks display　　77

6.1　Chicopee Public Library Bookmobile　　93

7.1　Photograph of computer trainer　　106

7.2　Clinician Cover Sheet　　113

7.3　Patient Cover Sheet　　113

7.4　PERC Packs Requested by Topic 2014　　115

7.5　PERC Pack Completions by Topic—April 2015　　115

8.1　Web form to collect desk statistics　　122

8.2　Levit Learning Center slat wall　　128

9.1　Seven Key Skills Sets　　137

9.2　Patient Activation Measure Levels　　138

TABLES

1.1　Selected Questions Answered in 2014–2015　　6

1.2　2014 Patient/Family Resource Center Timetable　　13

2.1　Preston Medical Library Summary of Best Practices　　31

6.1　Logic Model　　97

Preface

Health (and the health care industry) is in the news every day, from discoveries of new treatments for cancer, to fundraisers for diseases such as ALS (amyotrophic lateral sclerosis) or the Children's Miracle Network, to locating genetic markers for Alzheimer's, to almost daily discussion about the Affordable Care Act (Obamacare)—the talk about health care and the need to locate health care information abounds. Health and health care affects everyone, men and women, old and young. Whether looking for information about a disease (symptoms, treatments, genetics, etc.) or needing help in applying for health insurance online or trying to locate a doctor, most people, at one time or another, will need help in finding health care-related information.

Health care topics are among the most heavily searched topics on the Internet. According to the Pew Internet Project (2015), 87 percent of adults in the United States use the Internet (January 2014 survey), and of those, "72% of internet users say they looked online for health information within the past year" (2012 survey). Librarians must be prepared to offer programs and services to facilitate health information seeking by the general public or patients looking for health information for themselves or for those they care for. From public libraries to hospital and academic health sciences libraries, consumer health information (CHI) services have become a high priority.

The Medical Library Association's Consumer and Patient Health Information Section (CAPHIS) defines consumer health information as "information on health and medical topics provided in response to requests from the general public, including patients and their families. In addition to information on the symptoms, diagnosis and treatment of disease, CHI encompasses information on health promotion, preventive medicine, the determinants of health and accessing the health care system" (CAPHIS, 2013). The American Library Association's Reference & Users Services Association (RUSA) has developed guidelines that include provision of consumer health information, and the Medical Library Association offers a Consumer Health Information Specialization (https://www.mlanet.org/education/chc); the National Library of Medicine expanded its focus beginning in 1998 with the launch of the MedlinePlus consumer health website along with other products such as health assessment tools and MedlinePlus Connect. The interest in these organizations in consumer health information reflects the public's continued need for health information and the interest among both public and medical libraries in providing CHI to their constituents. *Consumer Health Information Services and Programs: Best Practices* offers advice and guidance for providing quality services and programs for all librarians who are looking to institute new programs or upgrade already existing services.

ORGANIZATION OF THE BOOK

Consumer Health Information Services and Programs: Best Practices features nine chapters, each of which offers advice, lessons learned, and best practices for providing health information to the general public and patients, from planning and establishing a CHI program to offering specialized services to special populations. Chapter authors were selected to provide a variety of unique and contemporary approaches and include librarians from hospitals, academic health science centers, and public libraries.

In chapter 1, "A Most ResourceFULL Consumer Health Information Center," Cara Marcus describes the services offered by the Patient/Family Resource Center (P/FRC) at Brigham and Women's Faulkner Hospital in Jamaica Plain, Massachusetts, which opened in 1999. The P/FRC provides reference services, Internet and wireless access, fax service, and free photocopying, and maintains a collection of resources that are fully vetted before being purchased. The library is open to anyone in the surrounding area. Marcus credits their success to customized, value-added service for each individual, quality resources, thoughtful analysis of organizational goals, and caring, friendly staff and volunteers.

Chapter 2, "The University of Tennessee Medical Center's Preston Medical Library and Health Information Center Story," describes the library's 1989 relocation and expansion, including the Consumer Health Information Service (CHIS). Sandy Oelschlegel, Martha Earl, and Kelsey Leonard document the development of the CHIS and emphasize best practices that include collaboration, assessment, outreach, staffing, collections, marketing, services, and research. Through funding from a grant, a new library was completed in 2014 that included the CHIS; a floor plan is included.

Health InfoNet of Alabama, begun in 1989, is a statewide, collaborative, free health information service for consumers comprised of the state's medical and public libraries. Chapter 3, "Health InfoNet of Alabama," by Kay Hogan Smith, describes the creation, organization, and implementation of this program, including services, funding, and marketing. Smith discusses survival "post-Go Local" (a program of the National Library of Medicine). Lessons learned include advice about funding, staffing, community outreach, and collaboration.

In chapter 4, "Consumer Health Information Service in the Public Library," Barbara M. Bibel describes the role of the public library in providing consumer health services, including the importance of providing access to current, reliable resources online and in print and the need to teach patrons how to use these resources. Appendices include a list of resources for materials in non-English languages, the ALA Library Bill of Rights, the ALA Code of Ethics, and the Code of Ethics for Health Sciences Librarianship.

Deidra Woodson and Donna F. Timm describe how an academic health sciences library provides collaborative programming with local public libraries in chapter 5, "Rewards and Challenges of Children's Health Education: An Ongoing Community Partnership to Reach Local Preschoolers." Using grant money from their regional library, the LSU Health Shreveport Health Sciences Library partnered with public librarians to provide story-time programs on health-related topics such as diet and exercise for children in their area. Lessons learned included: be flexible, be prepared for the unexpected, and be resourceful and creative. The long-term relationship with public libraries has been rewarding on both sides. An appendix has an extensive list of books to use for story times.

Another collaborative effort between a hospital library (Baystate Health in Massachusetts) and a public library (Chicopee Public Library) is described by Margot Malachowski, Anne Gancarz, and Ellen Brassil in chapter 6, "Collaborative Outreach between a Hospital Library and a Public Library." In addition to the medical library, Baystate Health (Massachusetts) operates a consumer health library (CHL) in Springfield. The authors describe services offered by the CHL along with their efforts to engage in community outreach, which resulted in a joint program with Chicopee Public Library. The collaborative effort, partially grant-funded, involved data analysis of community needs, which drove their selection of services. One major service was a new bookmobile. Best practices include building relationships and using available data.

In chapter 7, "Consumer Health and the Department of Veterans Affairs Library Network," Priscilla L. Stephenson, Teresa R. Coady, Diane

K. Kromke, Laurie A. Barnett, and Cornelia E. Camerer describe consumer health information services provided by the Department of Veterans Affairs Library Network (VALNET). CHI services are extensive and include "information prescriptions," service to outpatient clinics, outreach to Spanish-speaking veterans, and other services such as help with computer and information literacy and social networking support. Two case studies highlight the chapter—one involving the new library at the Orlando VA center and one about PERC (Patient Education Resources Center) packs. Best practices support patient-centered care for veterans.

Consumer health services at a specialized hospital are the focus of chapter 8, "The Learning Center: A Cancer Consumer Health Library at MD Anderson Cancer Center." Elizabeth Brackeen describes the services offered to patients and their families at their three Learning Centers. This "full-service" library is customer oriented, providing reference and circulation services to walk-in patrons and patients, emphasizing the importance of knowing as much as possible about a patient's diagnosis in order to provide the most accurate information. Best practices include making resources as accessible as possible to patrons and maintaining relationships and alliances within the institution.

In chapter 9, "The Big Health Library Umbrella: Our Mandate to Provide Information for All Literacy Abilities," Jackie Davis tackles the important concept of health literacy—the need to provide health information at the proper reading level to patrons and patients so that they can understand their own (or their family member's) health diagnosis and treatment. She describes how each librarian will need time and experience to develop the skills necessary to provide consumer health information. Best practices include collaborating with colleagues, taking continuing education courses, and locating free resources that provide proper reading levels. Davis challenges libraries and librarians to become involved in finding solutions for health literacy issues.

Throughout all of the chapters, you will find best practices provided by experienced librarians from all types of libraries—hospital, academic health sciences, government, and public libraries. Among the best practices you will find advice about are:

- funding opportunities;
- recommendations on how to evaluate services;
- ways to collaborate with library colleagues and with individuals and departments within and outside your organization;
- recommendations on selection of quality materials; and
- the need for friendly, service-oriented staff and volunteers.

The hope is to inspire current and prospective consumer health librarians with new ideas to implement creative CHI services and programs.

REFERENCES

CAPHIS (Consumer and Patient Health Information Section). Medical Library Association. 2013. "The Librarian's Role in the Provision of Consumer Health Information and Patient Education." Medical Library Association Policy Statement. Updated November 27. http://caphis.mlanet.org/chis/librarian.html.

Pew Internet Project. 2015. "Health Fact Sheet." Accessed October 4. http://www.pewinternet.org/fact-sheets/health-fact-sheet/.

Acknowledgments

I would like to thank all of the authors who contributed to this book (listed in chapter order): Cara Marcus, Sandy Oelschlegel, Martha Earl, Kelsey Leonard, Kay Hogan Smith, Barbara M. Bibel, Deidra Woodson, Donna F. Timm, Margot Malachowski, Anne Gancarz, Ellen Brassil, Priscilla L. Stephenson, Teresa R. Coady, Diane K. Kromke, Laurie A. Barnett, Cornelia E. Camerer, Elizabeth Brackeen, and Jackie Davis. These authors have shared their many years of experience in working with patrons searching for health information; their expertise will guide others who follow in their footsteps.

A Most ResourceFULL Consumer Health Information Center

CARA MARCUS, *Brigham and Women's Faulkner Hospital's Patient/Family Resource Center*

BACKGROUND AND SCOPE

Brigham and Women's Faulkner Hospital (BWFH) is a one-hundred-fifty-bed nonprofit, community teaching hospital located in Jamaica Plain, Massachusetts. The hospital established libraries for its doctors and nurses as soon as it opened in 1903. In 1931, the hospital founded the first official patient library, which was staffed by volunteers and consisted of donations of books and magazines. The current BWFH Patient/Family Resource Center (P/FRC) opened on September 27, 1999. At that time, it was one of the first community hospitals in Massachusetts to have a patient library ("Timeline," 2003). The P/FRC is located across from the hospital cafeteria on the third floor and is open between the hours of 9 AM and 3 PM, Monday through Friday. There is a full-time director, two part-time staff members, and about a dozen part-time volunteers.

A peaceful, quiet sanctuary where patients and families can read, relax, and learn as sunshine streams through the floor-to-ceiling windows, visitors are surrounded by tranquil plants and flowers and *Skyways*, a series of hanging serigraphs by artist Walter Darby Barnard. In Lindberg and Humphreys's (2005) vision of the future of medical libraries, they envisioned a future where users flock to library buildings that are attractive and the "library as place" is still highly valued. The P/FRC is meant to be a library that one can truly be comfortable in.

The P/FRC maintains a collection of the latest resources in the specialties the hospital serves and provides reference services, Internet and wireless access, fax service, and free photocopying. All materials are listed in an online catalog. The P/FRC's quarterly newsletter is aptly named *resource-FULLness* to highlight the breadth and depth of the resources offered.

The earliest recorded data on P/FRC utilization showed that slightly over 500 people visited in 2003 ("Usage," 2004). In 2014, there were 2,296 P/FRC users. The P/FRC currently carries over two hundred brochure titles, over a dozen newsletters and magazines, and about two hundred fifty books. Online resources include extensive consumer health databases, on-demand educational videos, education handouts through electronic patient portals, and a Nook consumer health e-book collection. In-depth consumer health information research services are provided to over two hundred requestors annually.

The P/FRC is open to anyone in the surrounding area, including hospital patients, families, staff, and volunteers. This free service helps people find current information on a variety of medical conditions, treatments, and general health issues. During the past fifteen years, the P/FRC has enhanced its resources, services, technologies, and outreach initiatives to best meet the consumer health information needs of the communities it serves.

MISSION STATEMENT

The mission of the Patient/Family Resource Center is to provide Brigham and Women's Faulkner Hospital patients, their family members and friends, staff, and the surrounding community with high-quality, up-to-date information and staff support to better understand the health issues that affect them and their loved ones.

GOALS AND OBJECTIVES

- To assist the Patient/Family Education Committee in selecting and producing hospital-approved consumer information resources.
- To assess the type of information a user is seeking and the most appropriate learning style for the user (i.e., other language).
- To provide a physical space for users to gather information on their health concerns in addition to online information.
- To provide excellent customer service in delivery of all library services, which includes adherence to hospital standards.
- To actively promote the P/FRC and services to patients, their families and friends, staff, and the surrounding community.
- To provide a peaceful, quiet environment for family and friends to wait for loved ones.

A WIDE ARRAY OF RESOURCES, SERVICES, AND PROGRAMS

The cornerstone of the Patient/Family Resource Center is its resources, which are collected *proactively* to reflect existing, expanded, and new hospital service lines and *reactively*, utilizing data on questions asked by P/FRC patrons on an annual basis. Staff anticipate patient education needs by communicating with all stakeholders on a regular basis, attending hospital meetings, and reviewing relevant literature to stay current on trends in consumer health. Konieczko (2003) found that the most successful libraries tailored their products and services by listening, observing and absorbing, and aligning offerings to their organization's business operations, challenges, and long-term goals, and Spatz (2001) stressed the importance of resources reflecting the particular needs of one's own health care community to build a dynamic consumer health collection. Patient/Family Resource Center staff have been involved in the hospital's Patient/Family Education Committee since its inception, which has helped the P/FRC align its patient education collection goals with that of the overall hospital. Review criteria were developed to assure that all resources provided by the Patient/Family Resource Center meet the highest quality standards.

BEST PRACTICES EVALUATION CRITERIA

Every resource provided by the center has been reviewed against the following guidelines:

- Authority—The author of the resource is a subject expert from a trusted and respected organization well known for excellence in the subject matter.
- Accuracy—Messages should be truthful, honest, and as complete as possible. Information provided should be factually accurate. Data and statistics need to be substantiated.
- Currency—In general, resources that have been published or updated within the last five years will be considered for the collection, unless an older title is well regarded as the definitive source for information of its kind. Information, data, recommendations, bibliographies, and references within all resources should reflect current research and knowledge.
- Literacy—Resources should be written at or below an eighth-grade reading level. Consumers without any medical background or training should be able to understand the content without assistance.
- Design—Resources should be well designed in terms of color, typography, and layout.
- Cultural Competence—Resources should be free of any discriminatory statements, stereotypes, or biases. Materials that are produced in multiple languages and formats for those with disabilities are actively sought for the collection.

The entire collection receives an annual review, and materials that are no longer current are removed. Clinical subject experts within the hospital are often asked to provide an expert review of new material being considered for the collection. The review is not solely based on a checklist—it also takes into account personal opinions on each resource based on careful reading by library staff, patient volunteers, and subject experts. Papadakos et al. (2014) stressed that the tacit knowledge gained through the experience of reviewing should be included as part of the collection development process. This approach takes considerable time and resources, but is worth it to create a stellar collection.

Resources are available on diseases and conditions, medications, surgeries, nutrition and exercise, hospitals and care facilities (nursing homes, assisted living, etc.), eldercare, end-of-life issues, and general wellness. Figure 1.1 shows BookTalk participants surrounded by some of the P/FRC's many books, e-books, brochures, and displays.

The P/FRC collection was entered into an integrated online catalog in 2003. A customized OPAC (Online Public Access Catalog) user guide was developed to help searchers use basic features, such as keyword and title searching, and advanced features like enhanced subject heading searching and power searching. The National Library of Medicine's MeSH (Medical Subject Headings) Classification System was adopted and staff added call numbers to the spines of books. Finding aids for consumers without knowledge of library classification systems or medical terminology included special color-coded shelf and spine labels for groups of books and brochures,

Figure 1.1.   A BookTalk in the Patient/Family Resource Center (Credit: Caitlyn Slowe)

such as cancer, diabetes, reference, and foreign language books. In 2009, a magazine/newsletter rack was purchased and the brochure display area was increased by about 15 percent. Bulletin board displays are designed and updated each month with resources available in the P/FRC to educate visitors on National Health Observances.

A directory was created to assist users with finding information from the best of the best in consumer health websites. The directory lists general health websites, such as MedlinePlus.gov, as well as suggested sites for patients and family members to find out about alternative medicine, cancer, diabetes, nutrition, digestive conditions, mental health, and other important topics. The directory includes sites for men, women, teens, older adults, and people who speak different languages. The directory is provided to all visitors who wish to perform their own web searches. P/FRC staff also use this directory to search for online health information for patients and families who are not able to perform their own web searches.

Extensive work has been undertaken to make the P/FRC accessible and comfortable to visitors with disabilities and special needs, including:

- Ergonomic chairs with tilt J-bars and twister arms. The chairs and arms can be fully adjusted to comfortable heights and tilts.
- Ergonomic workstation that can be manually raised or lowered to accommodate wheelchair users and those who are more comfortable standing.
- Adjustable keyboard trays and monitor arms.
- Screen magnifier/CCTV—Visitors with low vision or color blindness can read any print resource on a large LCD screen at the settings they need to read best.
- Selected books in 18-point type, the size tested by a legally blind volunteer and found easy to see and read.
- A full-page, light, hand-held, magnifier that enlarges the print of any resource up to two times.

In addition to the directory of recommended consumer health websites, the P/FRC has created a number of high-quality original resources based on visitor needs and requests, such as:

- a binder to help patients and families find services that they may need in Boston, such as taxis, car rentals, hospital shuttle schedules, hotels, pharmacies, restaurants, and fitness and wellness centers in the area;
- a support group guide for medical conditions such as arthritis, depression, Parkinson's disease, fibromyalgia, etc., in the greater Boston area, indexed by medical subject and city/town;

- takeaway bins with carefully selected web printouts written in plain language on many health topics;
- a collection of quick and healthy recipe clippings from consumer health magazines as well as a healthy cookbook with over one hundred recipes, *Flavors of Faulkner Hospital*, which was contributed to by P/FRC staff, volunteers, patients, and family members and was published by Morris Press in 2011;
- a list of Spanish-language brochures the P/FRC provides with English title translations, available by English title, Spanish title, and subject;
- a resource sheet about researching physician credentials through state and national organizations;
- a guide to local, regional, and national prescription assistance programs.

Creation of these specialized products has been a team effort; each product is updated at least every five years, and some are updated annually. Time is taken to verify every website and phone number in each of the resource guides the P/FRC produces.

The P/FRC staff is able to provide information and direction to other resources or services on all topics, using various locator tools such as directories, dictionaries, and physician and hospital guides as well as databases and approved websites. See table 1.1 for a list of some of the questions answered within the past year.

Table 1.1.   Selected Questions Answered in 2014–2015

How do breath carbohydrate and breath methadone tests measure gluten intolerance?	What are some caffeine-free substitutes for coffee?	Where can I find low-cost dental care?	What local support groups are available for people with chronic pain?
Do research studies show a link between migraine and depression?	Can you find any day programs for a young adult with Asperger's syndrome accessible by bus?	Is there a list of osteopaths practicing in the Boston area?	Is funding available for hearing aids for an elderly person?
What is the difference between a dietitian and a nutritionist?	Is there evidence for low-dose Naltrexone as a treatment for Parkinson's disease?	What causes trigger finger and how is it usually treated?	Are there traveling insulin coolers available that work longer than eighteen hours?

PROMOTION OF SERVICES

- Open houses in front of the cafeteria highlight topics like cholesterol and diabetes education. Each open house features a clinical expert to educate visitors and answer attendee questions.
- Every month the director of library services leads a BookTalk on one of the health and wellness books in the collection, on topics including exercise, nutrition, stress, relaxation, and more.
- A webpage on Brigham and Women's Faulkner Hospital's website provides information to the public.
- A quarterly newsletter (*resourceFULLness*) is published in print and electronic format. The print newsletter is displayed throughout the hospital and is delivered to every hospital practice.
- A monthly opt-in e-mail listserv of new resources is distributed to more than seventy individuals.
- Staff and volunteers make rounds to inpatient floors a few times each week, ask patients if they need information on any health topic, and then hand-deliver materials. Research has shown that volunteers rounding on hospital patient floors and working with the librarian to deliver information can empower patients in their health care, and increase their sense of value and collaboration with the health care team (Davis, 2013).
- A color bookmark includes hours, information about resources, and recommended websites. This bookmark is given to all hospital inpatients along with their welcome packet.
- A Quick Response (QR) Code was designed to link directly to the Patient/Family Resource Center website, so people with smartphones can scan the image and find out about hours, contact information, and events.
- Volunteers bring a cart to the inpatient areas and visit each patient with leisure-reading books, magazines, and smiles.
- The library director offers one-to-one orientations and tours for all new employees.
- BookTalks and signings of *Images of America: Faulkner Hospital* by library director Cara Marcus (Arcadia Publishing, 2010) were held at Borders Bookstore and in conjunction with Boston Public Library and Jamaica Plain Historical Society.

RESOURCES NEEDED FOR IMPLEMENTATION

Staff

With only a full-time director, a half-time assistant librarian, and a five-hour-per-week library assistant, the P/FRC is open thirty hours per week. The director also is responsible for the medical library and the hospital archives, which are located on a separate floor. With effective management and good teamwork and communication, the P/FRC operates smoothly and rarely has to close. The director checks in with staff when they first arrive to discuss any new projects and answer questions, and holds monthly meetings that include staff and volunteers. Given the largely part-time schedules of the staff, monthly staff meetings are held on rotating days, and volunteers are given the opportunity to work an extra day or flex their day on the day of a staff meeting.

Volunteers

The P/FRC maintains a loyal cadre of volunteers, including some that have remained for over a decade. They range from high school, college, and graduate students to retirees and part-time workers. Volunteers like Veda Chandwani, pictured in figure 1.2, help staff the P/FRC and locate and

Figure 1.2.   P/FRC volunteers are ready to help (Credit: Marian Deacutis)

provide resources for visitors. Although each volunteer is only expected to give a four-hour-per-week time commitment, library services volunteers accounted for over one thousand volunteer hours in 2013. P/FRC volunteers regularly visit the inpatient floors to meet the information needs of the patients who cannot physically visit the center. This service elicits requests for material that will help patients understand their medical conditions and treatments. Recently requests for reading materials have increased, as well as requests for specific documents such as health care proxies and newspapers in foreign languages.

Volunteers provide door-to-door service by delivering health information and books to patrons. They also post library flyers, act as greeters at library tables at health fairs, create original artwork for displays, contribute to newsletters, and write book and media reviews.

Community Partnerships

It takes a village to raise a child and it also takes one to implement any program of value to a community. Librarians in health care organizations can develop a patient-centered approach to care through a variety of relationships: with patients, the providers, and organizations (Zipperer, Gillaspy, and Goeltz, 2005). Brigham and Women's Faulkner Hospital's Patient/ Family Resource Center has benefited from strong partnerships within the hospital, the immediate community it serves, the state, and many other organizations and agencies.

The Patient/Family Resource Center convenes quarterly meetings with a multidisciplinary hospital advisory committee that includes leadership from medicine, surgery, psychiatry, nursing, allied health, and information systems. The committee advises on policy, strategy, new initiatives, and quality assessment.

The P/FRC director and staff regularly interface with hospital departments and serve on a number of BWFH committees that also provide patient education, such as the Community Health and Wellness Department, the Patient/ Family Education Committee, the Cultural Competence Steering Committee, and the Domestic Violence Steering Committee. BWFH's Community Health and Wellness Department arranged for the P/FRC director to deliver healthy aging BookTalks to groups of senior citizens who meet regularly at a local church. This department also holds an annual Community Health Fair in the hospital. The P/FRC sponsors a Health Fair table, giving people bookmarks, resource and website lists, and brochures that help them become better and wiser searchers and readers of health information. For example, a brochure from the National Institute on Aging, "Beware of Health Scams," tells people to beware of material that claims to cure a disease (such as arthritis or Alzheimer's disease) that hasn't been cured by medical science.

In an effort to raise awareness, encourage reading, and build a sense of team and community, the P/FRC worked with BWFH's Cultural Competence Steering Committee to sponsor an annual *One Book: One Hospital* program beginning in 2014. The first selection was *My Beloved World* by Sonia Sotomayor and the second was *Things Fall Apart* by Chinua Achebe. Patients and family members visit the P/FRC to read the book on the Nook or listen to it on the digital book player. The P/FRC staff assisted visitors with borrowing it from their town library or purchasing it online. The director of library services facilitated the book discussion sessions, which drew over one hundred attendees during its first year.

Another program the P/FRC works on together with the Cultural Competence Steering Committee is Martin Luther King Jr. Day. The Patient/Family Resource Center supplies handouts with memorable quotations by Dr. King, a fun word-search puzzle about his life and great works, and a history of MLK Day.

The P/FRC has worked on many collaborative projects with BWFH's Patient/Family Education Committee, such as hosting a special open house to provide education about a new on-demand Patient Education TV offering—The Wellness Network. The director of library services helped staff a table that showed how to access patient education channels on any computer or mobile device. Visitors left with TV guides and information on how to log in.

To best serve individuals with disabilities, the P/FRC has forged a strong relationship with the Perkins School for the Blind in Watertown, Massachusetts. Through the Perkins Institute Braille and Talking Book Library, the P/FRC has acquired a permanent loan of a book-on-tape player and obtains new digitized consumer health books each month for patients and family members to listen to. A recorded book format can be used by people with visual disabilities, as well as those who find it difficult to read or hold print books. This easy-to-use device plays digital talking book cartridges as well as downloadable talking books from the Library of Congress. The player is available in the center as well as by request to listen to the book of the month in patient rooms. The Perkins Institute Braille and Talking Book Library and Worcester Talking Book Library supplies the P/FRC with one large-print consumer health book each month. This book is available on the new books display shelf in the center for reading throughout the month. Another service received through the Perkins Institute Braille and Talking Book Library is Newsline, a telephone service that reads newspaper and magazine articles aloud to people with disabilities. Newspapers in this service include the

Boston Globe, *New York Times*, and *Wall Street Journal*. This service is also available from telephones at patients' bedsides. Through a Perkins Institute job training program, a blind volunteer has worked in the P/FRC and has added Braille shelf labels to all the brochure racks.

Brigham and Women's Faulkner Hospital Library Services is recognized as a member of the National Network of Libraries of Medicine/New England Region (NN/LM NER), which is affiliated with the National Library of Medicine (NLM). The P/FRC has leveraged the outstanding resources available through this source to provide resources and end-user training on MedlinePlus.gov, including their information in forty different languages, NIH Senior Health, ToxNet, and Genetics Home Reference. The library director and experts from NN/LM NER have provided classroom-style training and open houses on these and other resources. The P/FRC also carries *Medline-Plus Magazine* and a variety of bookmarks and handouts on consumer health resources from Medlineplus.gov.

The NN/LM NER recently featured the Patient/Family Resource Center programs in their online *NER'eastah* newsletter. Michelle Eberle, NN/LM NER Consumer Health Information Coordinator, highlighted the P/FRC's creative health information outreach program featuring national health observances from the National Health Information Center. NN/LM NER staff have supported these programs throughout the years and have introduced patients and families to resources on MedlinePlus, NIH Senior Health, and other National Library of Medicine databases.

Budget and Funding

While operational costs are part of the Department of Library Services budget, the Patient/Family Resource Center has been largely grant-funded, beginning with a large grant in 1999 to purchase the initial furnishings, equipment, and resources to open the center.

Unrestricted grant funding has enabled the Patient/Family Resource Center to update the collection and equipment, fund special programs such as open houses, and launch special initiatives, such as helping people with special needs better use the facilities by purchasing ergonomic chairs and computer workstations.

All royalty proceeds from *Images of America: Faulkner Hospital* by Cara Marcus (Arcadia Publishing, 2010) and *Flavors of Faulkner Hospital* (Morris Press, 2011) benefit the Patient/Family Resource Center, and enable the purchase of consumer health books, brochures, and resources for patients and family members. Donations from individuals have enabled the Patient/Family Resource Center to purchase a fax machine, set of encyclopedias, DVD player on a rolling cart with a selection of consumer health films, educational anatomic models of the body, and 3-D displays of healthy food portions.

One of the largest challenges has been to maintain and even expand product and service offerings with fewer budgetary resources each year. Utilizing Better World Books (a company that sells books donated by libraries and uses a portion of the proceeds to benefit literacy causes), both for donating older books and purchasing new books, has proved beneficial. Donating books, rather than throwing them away and adding to the landfill, also reaps environmental benefits. It was estimated that in one year, the Patient/Family Resource Center helped the environment by saving 677 gallons of water, 196 pounds of greenhouse gases, and 303 kilowatts of electricity, all by donating older books to Better World Books.

Timetable

Coordination of the P/FRC collection, events, and original publications requires careful planning, staff communication, and effective time management. Table 1.2 lists all the initiatives completed in 2014.

A PATIENT/FAMILY-CENTERED APPROACH

A library's staff is its most valuable asset. The greatest assembly of materials or virtual resources won't get a patient or family member far if the staff is unapproachable or unknowledgeable (Bandy and Dudden, 2011). P/FRC staff and volunteers are trained to warmly greet each visitor, ask if he or she needs any assistance, introduce any ready-reference materials on the shelves that may quickly answer the question, and work with the visitor to fill out a reference request form if the question cannot be answered during his or her visit. The center's motto is, "If it exists, we'll find it!" Completed research requests are mailed to requestors along with an evaluation form and self-addressed stamped envelope.

In addition to the promise that the staff and volunteers will make every effort to find the information that visitors (and telephone and e-mail requestors) need, everyone is trained on how to deliver customer service in a way that makes the visitor feel respected, understood, and valued. Patients and family members in a hospital are often wrestling with difficult and upsetting news, and a friendly face and kind words from someone who is helping them really does make a difference. User feedback from P/FRC surveys has focused on this important and often neglected aspect of service: the staff and volunteers were "very kind and caring," "spent a good deal of time helping me," and "really put in a lot of effort and listened to our concerns."

Table 1.2.   2014 Patient/Family Resource Center Timetable

January–March	April–June	July–September	October–December
Bound for Your Good Health BookTalk (1/8)	*Family Caregiver Handbook* BookTalk (4/9)	Magazine renewals	Fall Book Order
MLK Day Open House (1/20)	*Natural Health, Natural Medicine* BookTalk (5/14)	*One Health: Many Menus* BookTalk (7/9)	*Ferri's Netter Patient Advisor* BookTalk (10/8)
Planning for Uncertainty BookTalk (2/12)	Accessible Archives Onsite Online Class (5/15)	One Book: One Hospital Book Discussion Group (7/28)	One Book: One Hospital Book Discussion Group (10/17)
Heart Health Open House (2/18)	Community Health Fair (5/17)	*Embarrassing Medical Problems* BookTalk (8/8)	Bone and Joint Wellness Open House (10/21)
Field Guide to Germs BookTalk (3/12)	Skin Cancer Open House (5/20)	One Book: One Hospital Book Discussion Group (8/14)	*The Patient Survival Guide* BookTalk (11/12)
World Kidney Day Open House (3/13)	*I Need an Operation. Now What?* BookTalk (6/11)	*Prepare for Surgery, Heal Faster* BookTalk (9/10)	Digestive Health Open House (11/18)
Natural Standard Onsite Online Class (3/19)	Healthy Vision Open House (6/17)	Breast Cancer Open House (9/16)	*Encyclopedia of Foods: A Guide to Healthy Nutrition* BookTalk (12/10)
Deadline for Spring *resourceFULLness* newsletter (3/31)	One Book: One Hospital Launch Table (6/30)	One Book: One Hospital Open House (9/30)	Deadline for Winter *resourceFULLness* newsletter (12/31)
Spring Book Order. Update Brochures, Handouts, Original Publications	Deadline for Summer *resourceFULLness* newsletter (6/30)	Deadline for Fall *resourceFULLness* newsletter (9/30)	Plan Next Year's Events and Initiatives

ASSESSMENT

Research has shown that development and provision of resources and services to meet library customers' identified needs works best when based on data (Spatz, 2014). P/FRC staff assess programs quantitatively (number of visitors at events, number of questions asked, etc.), qualitatively (user satisfaction surveys and direct visitor feedback at point of service), and through systematic analyses of metrics surrounding annual quality goals.

A user satisfaction questionnaire is handed to all requestors and mailed out with literature searches with a stamped/self-addressed envelope. This survey collects feedback on whether a user's question was answered in full, the responsiveness of the staff, and the ability of users to find information using the center by browsing on their own. Open-ended questions collect data on users' perceptions of the P/FRC's most valuable resources and areas in need of improvement. The director compiles statistics monthly and annually and follows up with the library advisory committee on all user needs identified. In general, feedback has been quite positive, and feasible user needs (such as having a clock in the center) have been swiftly implemented.

To determine the adequacy of P/FRC resources to proactively answer questions, staff created a spreadsheet that mapped questions asked to the resources available on the shelves and on the list of recommended websites. For many of the frequently asked questions, such as those on breast cancer and Alzheimer's disease, there was already a wealth of resources. Staff were also able to use the data to identify new needs and obtain resources to fill those needs. This user-driven acquisitions quality project introduced a number of new resources into the P/FRC collection, such as *The New Mediterranean Diet Cookbook* and *Your Guide to Spinal Fusion*. Staff continue to monitor questions and collect relevant resources to answer them. Once a program is launched, gathering user feedback on a regular basis has been demonstrated to be important and valuable (Konieczko 2003).

EFFECT OF INITIATIVES ON LIBRARY SERVICES AND ROLE

The new initiatives implemented during the past ten years—BookTalks and Book Discussion Groups, customized resource guides, and accessibility for individuals with disabilities—have all served to enhance the experiences of Brigham and Women's Faulkner Hospital's Patient/Family Resource Center visitors. Many users return time and time again because they know they will receive personalized service, attentiveness to their individual health information needs, and quality resources that are customized to their questions.

Planning and implementing these resources and services is time consuming and requires skill, attentiveness, and commitment to detail. For example, if a patient asks for a list of support groups for arthritis near Boston, staff will search through all print and web-based resources to gather a list, and then call each one of the facilitators to verify the date/time/address/contact information. The result is a current, valuable resource list that the patient would not be able to find anywhere else. Volk (2007) demonstrated that providing more detailed information through expert searching than what is offered through basic, introductory materials (such as brochures and handouts) is a valuable role for health services libraries. At open houses, clinical experts volunteer their time to answer individual patient and family questions on the spot, or follow up with a detailed answer at a later time. Requesters can be assured that whatever their questions, language, level of literacy, ability or disability, the Patient/Family Resource Center will do whatever it takes to find answers.

NEXT STEPS

Brigham and Women's Faulkner Hospital has recently implemented an electronic health record system, which brings new learning opportunities for patients in terms of patient education handouts and interactive tools such as health trackers, as well as potentially more questions from patients about their medical conditions as they read through their chart. The importance of patient education has been demonstrated through research, and is required by federal regulatory agencies (Oelschlegel, Gonzalez, and Frakes, 2014). Patient/Family Resource Center staff and volunteers have all been trained on the patient portal, and will be able to help visitors find the information they need within this tool.

Over the past five years, there has been a definite increase in patient requests for literature beyond consumer health level information. Many patients now ask to see the original studies behind the news articles. Creating syntheses of clinical literature to be understood by the average consumer is one of the newest resources offered by the P/FRC, and this service is expected to gain momentum.

The Patient/Family Resource Center is always looking for more and better ways to get the word out about the services that it offers. New directions include providing copies of selected P/FRC research reports to staff who may be able to use them to refer patients to the center (such as social work, case management, etc.), increasing the number of embedded librarian sites throughout the hospital, and creating a branded P/FRC tablecloth for open houses and events.

BEST PRACTICES FOR OTHER LIBRARIES

Consumer health library managers can follow these suggestions to optimize their programs and resources.

- Anticipate user needs and create products and services for future requests. If a new law, like the Affordable Care Act, is passed, what questions may come up that your center may be able to answer? If your hospital is planning to develop a new practice, work with the planners to see how the center may be able to help their patients.
- Review every word in every resource. Don't judge a book just by its reviews—review it yourself. Obtain reviews from multiple perspectives (librarian, patient, clinical expert). Only include resources that satisfy all collection development criteria and are genuinely pleasant to read.
- Hold regular staff meetings to track progress, gain feedback on projects, and ensure ongoing communication. Include volunteers in staff meetings and trainings. The director and staff should have opportunities to attend external meetings, both within and beyond the organization.
- Offer staff and volunteers opportunities for learning and familiarization with the print and online collections. The more they know, the more they will be able to assist visitors.
- The consumer health library is part of the larger health care organization (hospital, health center, etc.). The director should meet regularly with key stakeholders so they know what the library can offer, and so he or she understands the organization's priorities and plays a role on the patient care team.

TAKEAWAYS

- Resources and services should be based on thoughtful analysis of data on organizational goals and identified needs of library users.
- The best services are those where the consumer health library can provide something value-added, unique, and customized for each and every individual.
- Quality is foremost. Reading every word of every resource and calling individuals to confirm services are time-consuming processes, but they are the only way to make sure that the resources meet quality goals.
- Kind, caring, and friendly staff and volunteers who truly care about patients and families are the cornerstone of an exemplary consumer health library.

CONCLUSION

Since 1999, Brigham and Women's Faulkner Hospital's Patient/Family Resource Center has provided over fifteen thousand patients and family members with thoughtfully selected resources to help them better understand their medical conditions and treatment options. Dedicated, skillful, and caring staff and volunteers serve as front line P/FRC representatives to provide individualized consumer health information consultations. As a recent P/FRC user stated, "I could not make good medical decisions without your help."

Technologies have changed dramatically during this time period, which has enabled the P/FRC to enhance offerings with resources in multiple formats for users who have different learning styles. Staff have conducted extensive data collection efforts to tailor services and programs to our community. Partnerships with key internal and external stakeholders have proved tremendously beneficial, and have enabled the P/FRC to provide resources in many languages and formats, for users of all abilities and disabilities. P/FRC leadership continues to look for ways to provide outreach, publicize services, learn, and grow. Recent programs, such as the Healthy Sleep Open House, pictured in figure 1.3, demonstrate how creativity and innovation can be used to promote consumer health information services. Whatever changes may transpire to the future consumer health landscape, resourceFULLness will always be our goal.

Figure 1.3.   Healthy Sleep Open House (Credit: Caitlyn Slowe)

REFERENCES

Bandy, Margaret M., and Roslind F. Dudden. 2011. *The Medical Library Association Guide to Managing Health Care Libraries*. New York: Neal Schulman Publishers.

Davis, Jackie. 2013. "Health Information Ambassador Program for Patient Education: A Best Practice for Bringing the Consumer Health Library to the Patient." *Journal of Consumer Health on the Internet* 17, no. 1: 25–34.

Konieczko, Jill. 2003. "Information Centers that Innovate: Six Librarians Provide Secrets to Success." *Information Outlook* 7, no. 1: 18.

Lindberg, Donald A. B., and Betsy L. Humphreys. 2005. "2015—the Future of Medical Libraries." *New England Journal of Medicine* 352, no. 11 (March 17): 1067–70.

Oelschlegel, Sandy, Ann Gonzalez., and Elizabeth Frakes. 2014. "Consumer Health Information Centers in Medical Libraries: A Survey of Current Practices." *Journal of Hospital Librarianship* 14, no. 4: 335–47.

Papadakos, Janet, Aileen Trang, David Wiljer, et al. 2014. "What Criteria Do Consumer Health Librarians Use to Develop Library Collections? A Phenomenological Study." *Journal of the Medical Library Association* 102, no. 2 (April): 78–84.

Spatz, Michele A. 2001. "Building the Dynamic Consumer Health Collection." *Journal of Hospital Librarianship* 1, no. 1 (March): 85–99.

Spatz, Michele A. 2014. *The Medical Library Association Guide to Providing Consumer and Patient Health Information*. Lanham, MD: Rowman & Littlefield.

"Timeline." 2003. *Patient/Family Resource Center Newsletter* 1, no. 1 (November): 3.

"Usage of the Patient/Family Resource Center Continues to Rise." 2004. *Patient/Family Resource Center Newsletter* 2, no. 2 (November): 2.

Volk, Ruti Malis. 2007. "Expert Searching in Consumer Health: An Important Role for Librarians in the Age of the Internet and the Web." *Journal of the Medical Library Association* 95, no. 2 (April): 203–7, e66.

Zipperer, Lori, Mary Gillaspy, and Roxanne Goeltz. 2005. "Facilitating Patient Centeredness through Information Work: Seeing Librarians as Guests in the Lives of Patients." *Journal of Hospital Librarianship* 5, no. 3 (September): 1–15.

## 2

The University of Tennessee Medical Center's Preston Medical Library and Health Information Center Story

SANDY OELSCHLEGEL, MARTHA EARL, KELSEY LEONARD,
Health Information Center/Preston Medical Library;
University of Tennessee Graduate School of Medicine;
The University of Tennessee Medical Center, Knoxville

The Preston Medical Library (PML) has provided a Consumer Health Information Service (CHIS) since 1989. Through conference presentations, published papers, outreach, and training programs to both consumers and libraries, Preston has gained a solid reputation for excellence in this service area. That reputation is not limited to the library community and the consumers served, but is also recognized by the University of Tennessee Graduate School of Medicine (UTGSM) and University of Tennessee Medical Center (UTMC) leadership. Further recognition of the impact of the library's service on health literacy and the potential for improved patient outcomes resulted in the UTMC and UTGSM supporting the relocation and expansion of the Preston Medical Library to the new Health Information Center (HIC). This chapter will describe the best practices that resulted in this move, including redefining the CHIS to meet the needs of East Tennessee patrons, utilizing statewide and local outreach projects to inform and promote the service, refining assessment methods, and promoting the importance of the service. The new library, services, and resources will be described, including funding mechanisms, design, and staffing.

BACKGROUND

The Preston CHIS began in 1989 when the library was the recipient of a Library Services and Construction Act (LSCA) grant from the Tennessee State Library and Archives (TSLA) in the amount of $6,000. This was the "first time that the Tennessee State Library provided financial support to a non-public library" (Rice, 1989: 1). The proposal, submitted by the director of the Preston Library at the time, stated, in part, that the "purpose of the proposed project is to develop a consumer health education collection as specified by the Medical Library Association, which would mesh with the technical collection already in heavy use at Preston Medical Library" (Yeomans, 1989: 4). Records indicate that the distribution of funds included: $4,000 used for monographs, which included titles at patient level, and $2,000 used for the acquisition of videotapes educating the consumer on health topics. This grant funding was the beginning of a twenty-five-year journey of developing the best practices described throughout this chapter and culminating in the opening of the new HIC.

In 1989, the CHIS was primarily a telephone-based service. The library worked closely with the Knox County Public Library (KCPL) system, taking referral calls from the public library for patrons whose questions went beyond the scope of the public librarian's knowledge or resources. Preston librarians conducted train-the-trainer classes for KCPL staff, which increased referrals. The class was approved by the TSLA for four hours of continuing education credit. Evaluation surveys from the classes identified the need from public librarians to collaborate with medical librarians as a best practice. Public library staff expressed a need for partnership, especially related to medical terminology, confidentiality, liability, outdated or incomplete sources, emotional issues, and privacy and literacy levels (Stephenson et al., 2004). The role of academic medical center librarians in training public librarians has been well established (Wessel, Wozar, and Epstein, 2003).

Medical librarians also provided consultation on collection development (Rees, 2000). Print materials did not circulate to consumers from Preston but could be requested through KCPL or the Area Resource Center at no charge with a limit of three requests per patron per month.

To facilitate this collaboration with KCPL, a brochure was developed and distributed to the Knox County Public Library branches. This practice of brochure development has persisted to today and remains a best practice for our setting. Additional promotion of the service in the early days included placement of brochures in doctors' offices and patient waiting areas, and advertising on television and on pharmacy bags of a local grocery store chain.

Patrons using the service during the early years when the Internet was not ubiquitous numbered one hundred per month (Earl, 1998). Those patrons could expect a packet of information to be compiled for pickup or mailed to them at their home. Sources used by librarians at that time included print resources, Gale's Health Reference Center, and some limited Internet resources. In addition, a grant from a local agency enabled PML to improve its consumer health book collection. The services were marketed primarily through print and television media, which continues to be a best practice.

NCLIS AWARD RECOGNITION

In 2004, the PML received recognition from the U.S. National Commission on Libraries and Information Science (NCLIS), which confirmed the success of the service. A letter from Beth Fitzsimmons, PhD, chairperson of the NCLIS, stated

> The University of Tennessee Preston Medical Library Consumer and Patient Information Service has been selected to receive the NCLIS Blue Ribbon Consumer Health Information Recognition Award for Libraries for Tennessee. The award is being presented to recognize the library for its efforts in providing accurate, useful consumer health information to the people of Tennessee, exemplifying the role libraries can play in increasing awareness of consumer health-related issues and encouraging healthy lifestyles. Both the direct delivery of health information to the consumer by the librarians at the Preston Medical Library, and the library's marketing efforts in bringing consumer health information to the community have enabled Tennessee to strengthen and build its consumer health information services, resulting in a healthier, well-informed community of users. Additionally, through the Preston Medical Library's training efforts for consumers and its train-the-trainer programs, the library staff serves as a resource and shares its expertise with a large body of users, epitomizing the concept of knowledge development and knowledge sharing, one of the basic tenets of professional librarianship. (NCLIS, 2005: 46)

The library continued to provide this service over the next decade, expanding and improving while using a number of outreach, assessment, and collaboration methods. Although the availability of the Internet impacted the number of calls, use of the services remained strong (Hodges and Johnson, 2009).

SERVICE EVALUATION

As the Internet became more widely available, the focus of the librarians at Preston turned to two areas: evaluating the needs of consumers and outreach to specific populations. The importance of evaluating library services using direct user input is emphasized by Burroughs and Wood as the best way to "establish a basic understanding about problems, satisfaction, and unmet information access needs of the community" (2000: 5).

Evaluation of the Preston CHIS service was accomplished in 1998, and again in 2009 using nearly identical survey tools (Earl, Oelschlegel, and Breece, 2012). The survey tool was based on validated questions previously used by Pifalo and colleagues (1997). The survey included twenty questions. Most were multiple-choice questions; however, space was provided for open-ended responses to encourage feedback. Included on the survey were questions about demographics, marketing efforts, customer satisfaction, and impact of information.

In both surveys, the satisfaction with the speed of delivery and quality of the information provided were overwhelmingly positive. In addition, the survey data indicated that the CHIS-provided information enhanced communications between respondents and their health professionals. There was also a positive impact on treatment, diagnosis, lifestyle habits, and attitude toward health. The greatest impact was on "your treatment" followed by "attitude toward health" and "lifestyle habits." Respondents were proactive regarding how the information they received affected their health care in the comments section. In both 1998 and 2009, the information received from the surveys was used to improve the services, focus the outreach needed to continue to promote the service, and ensure its value to the users.

The use of surveys as a method of evaluating the Preston CHIS was well established, but in August 2013, it was taken a step forward to be integrated into the service as a continuous quality-assessment tool. The new survey was developed based on the original validated surveys from 1998 and 2009. This survey is available in both a paper form and using Survey Monkey. A letter about the survey options is enclosed, along with the information requested through the CHIS. From August 2013 through September 2014, 279 surveys were completed. The survey was then altered due to the new location, but the practice of continuous quality assessment is ongoing. The surveys continue to show that the service is of high quality and has an impact on patient-physician communication, and on treatment, diagnosis, lifestyle habits, and attitude to health.

DEVELOPING OUTREACH

The need for assessment of library services is well established, but often not based on a systematic approach (Joubert and Lee, 2007). In 2003, Preston librarians began seeking a standardized way to assess the use of the CHIS across the region. Since the service was primarily based on mailing packets of information to people, zip codes offered a way to standardize the geographic aspects of each call. Additional standardization was achieved by applying the controlled vocabulary of the National Library of Medicine's MeSH terms to define each request.

In order to support the assessment, an SQL database was created of all calls made to the service since 1999. The database included the caller's name and address, the health topic, and MeSH term on which the caller requested information. The database has been kept current and can therefore be considered a best practice. The data have been used to evaluate the use of the service geographically by identifying specific geographic and socioeconomic groups to target for outreach. It has also been used to answer research questions and pursue funding. A number of projects have utilized the data and allowed Preston librarians to analyze the CHIS, some of which are listed below.

- Establish whether outreach events impacted the number of calls from specific zip codes (Oelschlegel, Earl, and Cole, 2006)
- Compare the rate of calls on specific diseases to the prevalence in the state (Green, Oelschlegel, and Earl, 2010)
- Use zip codes and U.S. census data to explore socioeconomic characteristics of users (Oelschlegel et al., 2009)
- Establish rates of calls by county to show value to medical center leadership
- Identify zip codes of populations not using the service to target outreach (Socha et al., 2012)

EVALUATION OF HEALTH INFORMATION NEEDS ACROSS THE STATE

In 2005, funding was received through the National Network of Libraries of Medicine, Southeastern/Atlantic (NNLM/SEA) Region Outreach State Planning and Evaluation Award for PML to form a statewide team to examine the existing health information resources and services available for distribution of health information for consumers. Another goal was to assess the need for these services in order to identify opportunities for service expansion and partnerships for the future.

The goals of the project were to be reached during a series of two meetings and through the distribution and analysis of a needs-assessment tool. Invited participants of the meetings included representative(s) from NN/LM-designated state-funded resource libraries, the Tennessee Health Sciences Libraries Association, the state resource sharing group, major public libraries, the Tennessee State Library and Archives, state agencies (public health, rural health, etc.), and health professionals' state associations.

The objectives included completing a statewide health information needs assessment and identifying existing resources, services, and key stakeholders in the state for future partnerships and collaborations. Based on the needs assessment, a plan for meeting the future health information needs of the state was developed.

As another example of best practices for creating collaborations, this project was very successful. It not only identified the health information needs through the assessment, but it also created partnerships across the diversity of participants (Oelschlegel, Ponnappa, and Due, 2006).

OUTREACH TO LIBRARIES

Several projects that came out of the statewide planning sessions were notably successful and could be considered best practice due to their results. One of the outcomes was the recognition of the effectiveness of an outreach method started by East Tennessee State University (ETSU), which became referred to as the "Simple Plan" (Carter and Wallace, 2007). This outreach activity was focused on public libraries and based on the idea that medical librarians could train public librarians to more effectively provide consumer health services in their libraries. This would place access to health information at the front lines within each community.

The expansion of the Simple Plan in 2008–2009 was done by identifying the focal points of need after data assessment and communicating the needs at the highest level of the organization of the state's libraries. Data from the health information needs assessment, which was completed as part of the Outreach State Planning and Evaluation Award, were compiled showing that public librarians who responded to the survey expressed the need for training on how to provide health information to their patrons and how to practice collection development in the consumer health subject area. This information was presented at the State Librarian's meeting of the Regional Library directors. The participants unanimously accepted the proposal for a statewide expansion of the Simple Plan ("Tennessee Special Libraries Share Their Resources," 2008).

When another award was received from NNLM/SEA, the focus was on continuing and expanding the Simple Plan concept to the entire state. Preston librarians and ETSU librarians coordinated to provide classes to each of the ten regional library systems (Earl and Vaughn, 2010).

FAR OUT OUTREACH—TAKING IT TO SOUTH AFRICA

In 2011, as a measure of the Simple Plan's success, Preston librarians were invited to take the Simple Plan to South Africa (Earl, 2012). The two-week outreach project, jointly funded by the U.S. Embassy and the Library and Information Association of South Africa (LIASA), provided the Simple Plan classes to 310 people in thirteen classes in eleven library locations from Johannesburg to Cape Town (Earl et al., 2013).

Follow-up with the U.S. Embassy contacts identified that, as in Tennessee, public librarians did not feel confident to train other staff or the public without support from health sciences librarians. U.S. Embassy officials and LIASA leaders contacted Preston librarians to return to lead a three-day national summit, including brainstorming, regional collaboration, and practice teaching sessions, to connect health sciences and public librarians. Each attendee agreed to present an outreach class within six months of attending the workshop (Earl et al., 2014).

Similar to the Tennessee Outreach State Planning and Simple Plan projects, the resulting strategic planning carried forward a best practice model from Tennessee to South Africa. The result was partnerships of empowered librarians improving health literacy at the point of need.

OUTREACH TO BUSINESSES

Preston librarians were contacted in 2012 by the National Library of Medicine, Division of Specialized Information Services, and asked to develop a toolkit to serve as a model for other medical libraries to use in partnering with businesses. The goal of the project was to encourage corporate employee benefits staff to promote NLM and NIH resources to participants in employee wellness programs. After meeting with a corporate partner, Preston librarians developed a series of newsletter pieces, biometric screening-specific handouts, "Your Wellness Moment" video files, and a LibGuide of Internet resources. A toolkit for librarians outlined the successful methods for identifying and contacting appropriate corporate personnel and for creating outreach materials. The toolkit includes sample outreach materials that are available for download (Oelschlegel and Gonzalez, 2014).

REDEFINING THE MEDICAL LIBRARY
AS THE HEALTH INFORMATION CENTER

The idea for a health information center came about in 2009, with the intent to provide health education to patients and their families in a dedicated space. Due to the long history and success of PML's CHIS, and the library's ability to demonstrate value with data, hospital leadership invited the library to relocate within the hospital (Oelschlegel, Gonzalez, and Frakes, 2014). With the help of UTMC's CEO and the Dean of UTGSM, enough philanthropic dollars were raised to make this idea a reality. The HIC, along with PML, was built adjacent to the main lobby and opened in September 2014.

PLANNING THE NEW LIBRARY

In preparations for the relocation and expansion of the library, Preston librarians distributed a survey to medical libraries in order to evaluate patient-family-centered space and services to determine what best practices were in place. Three hundred six medical libraries responded to the survey from forty-six states and Puerto Rico. Respondents included 199 libraries (65 percent) with Consumer Health Information centers or services. Of those, 30.7 percent did not have a designated space, 57.1 percent had less than 1,000 square feet, and 12.1 percent exceeded 1,001 square feet. This space assessment allowed us to create a national benchmark from which the new facility could be planned. Additionally, it identified PML's HIC as one of the 12 percent that have a designated space of 1,001 square feet or more (Oelschlegel, Gonzalez, and Frakes, 2014).

Various services were also evaluated through the survey. Participants ranked the onsite reference desk and telephone reference as the most important services, while the highest-ranked outreach service was bedside delivery of health information. Internet access ranked as the most important electronic service. Consumer-level books were ranked the most important component of the physical collection. By reviewing the ranking of various services, librarians were able to plan for the future.

The survey also informed the staffing plans. Most libraries reported employing one or two professional librarians (81.5 percent), non-MLS staff were employed in 53.1 percent, and volunteers in 57.5 percent. These data were utilized in planning for three new positions, two non-MLS staff and one librarian, and for changing the job descriptions of existing personnel.

The HIC and PML were built in one contiguous space, with the reference desk serving both patron groups. A clever floor plan and design elements keep the public and academic library spaces separated visually and functionally ("Health Information Center Virtual Tour," 2015). Two entrances exist, one of which is designed for health care professionals and learners to enter and exit the library without passing through the designated public space, yet they still pass by the centrally located reference desk for ease of access to library personnel (see figure 2.1 floor plan).

The HIC has dedicated a space of over sixteen hundred square feet for patients, their families, and the community. Glass walls encompass the space to allow for visibility from the main hall of the hospital (see figure 2.2). The single point service desk, café tables, and comfortable seating are highly visible.

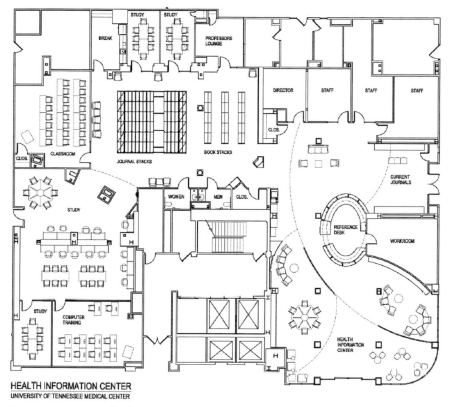

Figure 2.1.   UT Medical Center Health Information Center floor plan

Figure 2.2.   View of the UT Medical Center Health Information Center from lobby

The six public computers are equipped with high-speed Internet, which allows access to health and wellness databases. The consumer book collection is prominently displayed, as is a brochure wall that provides patients with further information regarding UTMC physicians and services (see figure 2.3). Throughout the entire space, wireless Internet access is available for those who prefer to use their own laptop, tablet, or smartphone.

As a best practice to guide the selection of books for the HIC, a collection development policy was written. The policy outlines the selection of books to be aligned with the diseases most prevalent in Tennessee and those diseases that fall within the scope of the six centers of excellence of the UT Medical Center. When selecting the materials, the leadership of each Center of Excellence was contacted in order to establish what they preferred to be a part of the collection. The books they suggested were reviewed and selected based on the new consumer collection development policy. Reading level of the books was especially important when choosing the materials. The books selected were between fifth- and eighth-grade reading levels. This decision was based on data that showed that Americans read at an average level of eighth to ninth grade, and one out of five Americans read at a fifth-grade level (National Patient Safety Foundation, 2011). The initial cost of the collection was limited to $5,000, but funds are available to continuously update it in order to allow for relevant and current materials.

Figure 2.3.   Patient-centered space and book collection at UT Medical Center Health Information Center

Patrons interested in checking out books can become a member of the HIC by completing a brief form that includes an agreement to return material. This form and a valid ID card are all that is needed for the HIC staff to set up a patron record. The membership list will also be used to stay connected to this patron group through mailings to invite them to events.

The staffing of the HIC is critical in order to provide services to both the public and academic medical patrons. A new librarian position for a "Health Information Services Librarian" and two part-time non-MLS staff were filled prior to opening. The new personnel are assigned to evenings and weekends. In order to maintain the excellent level of customized service for both patron groups, both the Medical Library Association's (MLA) Academy of Health Information Professionals (AHIP) and Consumer Health Information Specialization (CHIS) are required for librarians. All other personnel are required to have MLA CHIS Level One to ensure that they are trained to research health topics for patients and their family members. The CHIS is designed to keep staff and librarians current in the consumer health information field and document attendance in classes through a series of certificate levels (MLA, 2015b). The AHIP program is a peer-reviewed professional development and career recognition program for librarians that assigns members to various levels according to documentation of achievements through the application process (MLA, 2015a). In order to make certain that adequate staffing is available, a system was developed that maintains two personnel at the desk at all times, with an additional person scheduled as "backup." The backup is required to be present and available to assist. There is always one librarian on the schedule to handle clinical literature searches.

The HIC also offers resources online. Items listed on the homepage include information about the HIC, the health information service, classes offered, and research LibGuides created specifically for each of the Centers of Excellence. Patients, family members, and the community can easily request health information from that page. They can also sign up for one of the many classes offered by librarians. In addition, there is a page specifically for the collections, which not only includes the print books, but also the online databases.

The health information service, also known as the CHIS, is available for patients, their family members, and the community. These patrons can visit, call, e-mail, use web forms, text, or chat with library personnel to ask for health topics to be researched for them. They can even request information from the hospital bed. The health information service gives patients easy-to-read materials that relate to a recent diagnosis, medication, or procedure, which can help improve their understanding of their health care.

In PML's 2013 survey of medical libraries, bedside delivery of health information was shown to be one of the most important services a medical library can offer (Oelschlegel, Gonzalez, and Frakes, 2014). Skylight, an in-room television service that provides access to cable, movies, and Internet, was implemented hospital-wide in 2011 (Vaughn, Leonard, and Oelschlegel, 2014). During that time, the library partnered with the Patient Education Committee to allow patients to request health information via Skylight (Vaughn, Leonard, and Oelschlegel, 2014). The service has been marketed in a number of ways. To patients, it was marketed through a description in the "Visitor Guide," a display on the patient's television at 9:30AM and 4:30 PM, and laminated flyers in patient rooms. To nurses, the service was marketed by presenting at nursing shared governance councils, nurses huddles, and Nursing Grand Rounds.

Charting Patient Education

Once the patient alerts the library of their health information need using Skylight, a librarian calls their room to complete a reference interview. The librarian then delivers that information to the Health Unit Coordinator. In 2015, librarians began to chart the delivery of health information to patients in the electronic medical records. Library personnel have been given access to the electronic medical records in order to chart the topic of the information sent to the patient. The charting results in the creation of a task on the nurse's task list for that shift. The nurse then delivers the information to the patient, ensures comprehension, and notes any barrier to understanding, which is a requirement of the Joint Commission. With this new integration, the Preston librarians anticipate an increase in the number of Skylight health information alerts.

Utilization

The HIC has been operating for six months and has been very successful. Compared to the previous six months, there has been an 87 percent increase in door count, 30 percent increase in health professionals and learner transactions, and a 217 percent increase in transactions for patients, family members, and the community. The HIC has had sixty-seven patrons from the community join as HIC members and ninety-five books have been circulated.

Survey results are continuing to prove that the HIC is employing successful practices in providing health information services. Among the responses are two that highlight our impact, with 78 percent of respondents planning to use the information received to discuss with their doctor and 67 percent planning to use the information received to improve their health.

While these numbers are important, it is the stories behind the numbers that really speak to the quality and impact of the services provided in the HIC. Glimpses of these stories can be seen in the comments section of surveys, such as:

- These are fantastic services, resources and website. The facility is very inviting, informative and reminds me of being on a cruise ship. So great for a hospital!
- What an amazing place with great people who share excellent resources.
- I am thrilled to have found this service and I can't believe it's free. I tell everyone I know about it and your staff is genuine, caring, professional and extremely helpful. Kudos all.

Table 2.1 summarizes best practices gained from the experiences at the Preston Medical Library.

Table 2.1. Preston Medical Library Summary of Best Practices

Collaboration	State Library and Archives
	Knox County Public Library
	Clinicians and nurses
Assessment	Evaluation of the Preston CHIS service using validated survey tool
	Instituting a continuous quality-assessment survey
	National survey to establish benchmarks of medical libraries providing CHIS
Research	Using MeSH to evaluate the information needs of users
	Using zip codes and GIS software to evaluate the use of service through the region
	Using zip codes and GIS software to explore the socioeconomic characteristics of users
	Using zip codes and GIS software to discover health information disparities for outreach
Outreach	Statewide outreach state planning and evaluation
	Statewide training of public librarians to provide consumer health
	Introduction of CHIS methods to South Africa
	Work with corporate employee benefits staff to promote NLM and NIH resources.
Staffing	Required Academy of Health Information Professional (AHIP) credentialing
	Required MLA Consumer Health Information Specialization (CHIS)
	Reference Desk staffing using the backup system
Collection	Development of a separate policy for Health Information Center collection
	Aligned collection to the UT Medical Center's Six Centers of Excellence
	Reading level between fifth- and eighth-grade

(continued)

Table 2.1. *Continued*

Collection	Use of MLA Collection Development and CAPHIS Section lists
(*continued*)	Review of public library collection: Knox County Public Library
	Used *Library Journal, Kirkus, Publishers Weekly*, and other reviews sources
Services	Multiple communication points—Chat, e-mail, phone, web forms
	Patient-initiated, technology-assisted bedside delivery of health information
	EMR documentation of delivery and patient comprehension of health information
Marketing	Brochure
	Electronic and print hospital newsletter
	Social media
	Press release
	Television news spots

CONCLUSION

Application of best practices in providing a CHIS for over twenty years resulted in the relocation and expansion of Preston Medical Library. Best practices include needs assessment and evaluation of services. This allowed PML to redefine the CHIS to meet the needs of the Eastern Tennessee community and expand the impact of the services to the state and beyond.

REFERENCES

Burroughs, Catherine M., and Fred B. Wood. 2000. *Measuring the Difference: Guide to Planning and Evaluating Health Information Outreach.* Seattle, WA: National Network of Libraries of Medicine, Pacific Northwest Region.

Carter, Nakia J., and Richard L. Wallace. 2007. "Collaborating with Public Libraries, Public Health Departments, and Rural Hospitals to Provide Consumer Health Information Services." *Journal of Consumer Health on the Internet* 11, no. 4: 1–14. doi. 10.1300/J381v11n04_01.

Earl, Martha. 1998. "Caring for Consumers: Empowering the Individual." *American Libraries* 29, no. 10: 44–46. http://www.jstor.org/stable/25635192.

Earl, Martha. 2012. "UT Medical Librarians Teach Consumer Health Information in South Africa." *Medical Library Association Collection Development Section News* (Fall/Winter). http://colldev.mlanet.org/developments/ut-medical-librarians-tech-consumer-health-information-in-south-africa/.

Earl, Martha, Sandy Oelschlegel, and Alisa Breece. 2012. "Impact of a Consumer and Patient Health Information Service on User Satisfaction, Attitudes, and Patient-

Health Care Professional Interactions." *Journal of Consumer Health on the Internet* 16, no. 2: 192–212. doi. 10.1080/15398285.2012.673460.

Earl, Martha, and Cynthia Vaughn. 2010. "A Simple Plan Extended." *Tennessee Libraries* 60, no. 1. http://www.tnla.org/?page=354.

Earl, Martha F., Cynthia J. Vaughn, Mark L. Dobson, Naomi E. Haasbroek, and Steven P. Kerchoff. 2013. "South Africa One Year Later: Follow-Up and Outcomes from Outreach and Partnerships." Contributed poster presented at the Annual Meeting of the Medical Library Association, Boston, MA, May 3–8.

Earl, Martha F., Cynthia J. Vaughn, Naomi E. Haasbroek, Mark L. Dobson, and Steven P. Kerchoff. 2014. "Making a Difference in the Global Community: An Action Workshop Model." Contributed poster presentation at the Annual Meeting of the Southern Chapter of the Medical Library Association, Mobile, AL, October 26–30.

Green, David W., Sandy Oelschlegel, and Martha Earl. 2010. "Using ArcMap to Evaluate a Library Outreach Service." Contributed poster presented at the Annual Meeting of the Southern Chapter of the Medical Library Association, Petersburg, FL, November 12–16.

"Health Information Center Virtual Tour." 2015. *UT Medical Center.* Accessed May 20. http://www.utmedicalcenter.org/Health-Information-Center.html.

Hodges, Kandi, and Amanda Johnson. 2009. "Preston Medical Library Impacts Libraries, Families, and Rural Doctors." *Frontiers* (Spring).

Joubert, Douglas J., and Tamera P. Lee. 2007. "Empowering Your Institution through Assessment." *Journal of the Medical Library Association* 95, no. 1 (January): 46–53. http://www.ncbi.nlm.nih.gov/pmc/articles/PMC1773025/.

MLA (Medical Library Association). 2015a. "Academy of Health Information Professionals (AHIP)." Medical Library Association. https://www.mlanet.org/academy/.

MLA (Medical Library Association). 2015b. "Consumer Health Information Specialization." Medical Library Association. https://www.mlanet.org/education/chc.

National Patient Safety Foundation. 2011. "Health Literacy: Statistics At-A-Glance." National Patient Safety Foundation. http://c.ymcdn.com/sites/www.npsf.org/resource/collection/9220b314-9666-40da-89da-9f46357530f1/AskMe3_Stats_English.pdf?hhSearchTerms=%222011+and+ask+and+3+and+stats%22.

NCLIS (National Commission on Libraries and Information Science). 2005. *Libraries and Health Communication: Model Programs in Health Information Provided by Libraries throughout the Nation: The 2004 NCLIS Blue Ribbon Consumer Health Information Recognition Awards for Libraries.* Washington, DC: NCLIS.

Oelschlegel, Sandy, Martha Earl, and Jenny Cole. 2006. "Data Analysis of Consumer and Patient Health Questions Using Geographic Location and NLM Medical Subject Headings." *Hypothesis: Journal of the Research Section of MLA* 20, no. 1: 3. http://research.mlanet.org/hypothesis/hyp06v20n1.pdf.

Oelschlegel, Sandy, Martha Earl, Melanie Taylor, and Robert A. Muenchen. 2009. "Health Information Disparities? Determining the Relationship between Age, Poverty, and Rate of Calls to a Consumer and Patient Health Information Service." *Journal of the Medical Library Association* 97, no. 3 (July): 225–27. doi. 10.3163/1536-5050.97.3.013.

Oelschlegel, Sandy, and Ann B. Gonzalez. 2014. "Promoting National Library of Medicine and National Institutes of Health Resources to Industry: Developing a Wellness Outreach Toolkit." *Journal of Consumer Health on the Internet* 18, no. 3: 238–52. doi. 10.1080/15398285.2014.932179.

Oelschlegel, Sandy, Ann B. Gonzalez, and Elizabeth Frakes. 2014. "Consumer Health Information Centers in Medical Libraries: A Survey of Current Practices." *Journal of Hospital Librarianship* 14, no. 4: 335–47. doi. 10.1080/15323269.2014.950133.

Oelschlegel, Sandy, Suresh Ponnappa, and Kay Due. 2006. "Tennessee Outreach State Planning and Evaluation Team." Unpublished Report to National Network of Libraries of Medicine, Southeastern Atlantic Area (NNLM/SEA), Preston Medical Library Knoxville, TN.

Pifalo, Victoria, Sue Hollander, Cynthia L. Henderson, Pat DeSalvo, and Gail P. Gill. 1997. "The Impact of Consumer Health Information Provided by Libraries: The Delaware Experience." *Bulletin of the Medical Library Association* 85, no. 1 (January): 1–22. http://www.ncbi.nlm.nih.gov/pmc/articles/PMC226218/.

Rees, Alan M. 2000. *The Consumer Health Information Source Book.* Phoenix, AZ: Oryx Press.

Rice, Bill. 1989. Letter to employee Lynne Yeomans. September 12.

Socha, Yvonne M., Sandra Oelschlegel, Cynthia J. Vaughn, and Martha Earl. 2012. "Improving an Outreach Service by Analyzing the Relationship of Health Information Disparities to Socioeconomic Indicators Using Geographic Information Systems." *Journal of the Medical Library Association* 100, no. 3 (July): 222–25. doi. 10.3163/1536-5050.100.3.014.

Stephenson, Priscilla L., Brenda F. Green, Richard L. Wallace, Martha F. Earl, Jan T. Orick, and Mary Virginia Taylor. 2004. "Community Partnerships for Health Information Training: Medical Librarians Working with Health Care Professionals and Consumers in Tennessee." *Health Information and Libraries Journal* 21: 20–26. doi. 10.1111/j.1740-3324.2004.00498.x.

"Tennessee Special Libraries Share Their Resources." 2008. *Tenn-Share News.* http://www.tenn-share.org/node/117.

Vaughn, Cynthia, Kelsey Leonard, and Sandy Oelschlegel. 2014. "Delivery of Information to the Patient Bedside Utilizing Skylight In-Room Television Service." *Journal of Hospital Librarianship* 14, no. 1: 1–13. doi. 10.1080/15323269.2014.859880.

Wessel, Charles B., Jody A. Wozar, and Barbara A. Epstein. 2003. "The Role of the Academic Medical Center in Training Public Librarians." *Journal of the Medical Library Association* 91, no. 3 (July): 352–60. http://www.ncbi.nlm.nih.gov/pmc/articles/PMC164399/.

Yeomans, Lynne L. 1989. "Proposal for a Consumer Health Information Center to Support the State-Wide Area Resource Centers." Tennessee Department of State, Library Services and Construction Act Grant Proposal, Preston Medical Library, University of Tennessee Medical Center, Knoxville, TN.

3

Health InfoNet of Alabama

KAY HOGAN SMITH, *Lister Hill Library of the Health Sciences,*
University of Alabama at Birmingham

Health InfoNet of Alabama is a free consumer health information service of the state's medical and public libraries. Through this collaborative effort, the libraries offer in-person, online (via chat or e-mail), and telephone reference assistance for users with health questions. The aim is to steer users to reliable, current sources of information relevant to their needs. Along the way, the partnering librarians educate users about search methods as well as the importance of critically evaluating sources. This chapter will cover the creation, organization, and implementation of the Health InfoNet program, providing lessons learned along the way about best practices for this type of collaborative consumer health information project.

BACKGROUND

Health InfoNet started in the late 1990s as Health InfoNet of Jefferson County, focused primarily on the state's largest metropolitan area, Birmingham. Local medical librarians at the University of Alabama at Birmingham's Lister Hill Library of the Health Sciences noticed that a number of patients from the hospitals surrounding the library were making their way to Lister Hill to find out more about their diagnoses and treatments. While Lister Hill Library has always been open to the public, its primary focus was on serving the University's seven health profession schools, including medicine, optometry, dentistry, nursing, health professions, graduate biomedical sciences, and public health disciplines. The library collections had relatively few resources geared toward lay readers, and the Internet was, of course, in its infancy at the time. Using suggestions from Rees's book, *Managing Consumer Health In-formation Services* (1991), and with the partnership of local public librarians, a new consumer health information service built on the Connecticut Health-Net model was formed. The organization featured a collaborative approach among the medical and public libraries focusing on a medical reference train-ing and health collections consultation role of the medical libraries, and the establishment of an advisory committee consisting of health care providers, librarians, and other community representatives to provide guidance.

The first step, however, was to investigate the need for this service. To that end, the library partners set up a twofold needs assessment. First, a survey was devised to determine the need for such a service among health information providers including librarians, health care providers, and local health agencies, such as the Birmingham Planned Parenthood organiza-tion and the Sickle Cell Disease Association of America (Central Alabama Chapter). This survey was mailed in early summer 1998. Out of approxi-mately 233 surveys sent out, 118 were returned, a return rate of about 51 percent overall (88 percent return from libraries, 40 percent return from other information providers). The vast majority of respondents (75 per-cent) indicated that they did routinely provide at least some level of health information service to patients and families and/or the general public. The requestor of such information was most likely to be a patient or family member of a patient, according to the respondents. Although a few of the hospital libraries and voluntary health agencies indicated that they felt self-sufficient enough to handle most consumer health requests themselves, the majority (76 percent) of respondents stated that they "felt a need for help in responding to requests for information," or stated that they sometimes had to refer such requests to Lister Hill Library or the Birmingham Public Library. Of the libraries that responded, it was significant that 42 percent of the medical libraries rated their own consumer health collections as average or poor while 44 percent of the public libraries did the same.

The second part of the needs assessment focused on the target users of such a service. Since mailed surveys were considered impractical, it was decided that targeted focus groups would be the best way to obtain feedback from potential users of this service. (Online surveying technology was not widely available at the time.) Fortunately, the University of Alabama at Birmingham School of Public Health sponsored a "Survey Research Unit" within its Center for Health Promotion. This research unit agreed to host a series of seven focus groups (UAB, 2000) in late 1998 and early 1999, each one targeting a specific demographic group, for example black females 50 and above. (There was a nominal charge for this service, which UAB Lister Hill Library covered.)

The report from the focus groups highlighted specific findings, such as:

- Almost all of the participants needed health information at some point, usually relating to their own or a loved one's health concerns.
- The most frequently mentioned topics of interest included diet, exercise, diabetes, cancer, and hypertension.
- Participants' experience with the Internet for searching for health information varied widely. Those with little or no experience desired training in techniques for finding online health information.
- Only a few participants used libraries regularly, and most of them did not search for health information in the library.
- Those participants who were library users generally held the library services and staff in high regard.

The results of the surveys and focus groups confirmed the need for a new health information service based within the local public libraries with the support and training of the UAB Lister Hill Library of the Health Sciences. With more than forty public libraries and branches throughout the metropolitan Birmingham area, residents would be able to find ready assistance and resources for their health questions within their neighborhoods with this service.

The initial exploratory meeting of the Health InfoNet advisory committee was held in January 1999. This meeting included individuals who represented the following entities:

- Children's Health System
- Birmingham Public Library
- Jefferson County Health Department
- UAB Lister Hill Library of the Health Sciences
- Planned Parenthood of Alabama, Inc.
- Jefferson County Library Cooperative
- City of Birmingham
- UAB Medicine
- National Multiple Sclerosis Society, Central Alabama Chapter

Guidelines for the advisory committee stipulated that there should be nine committee members with representatives of the three cooperating libraries maintaining a permanent presence on the advisory panel. The others were to serve staggered terms to encourage a blend of experience and fresh enthusiasm on the panel.

The mission statement was drafted in January of 1999 and later revised to read as follows: "Health InfoNet provides access to high quality health information that is accurate, timely, unbiased and relevant to the citizens of Alabama" (Health InfoNet of Alabama, 2011).

ORGANIZATION

One concern expressed early by the newly formed advisory panel was that of Health InfoNet's nonprofit status and eligibility for funding. Establishing the project as a 501(c)3 nonprofit would open opportunities for funding as well as affirm its status among potential partners and backers as a worthy organization. On the other hand, the process for obtaining the IRS nonprofit status as a separate entity was daunting, and its successful completion might create other unintended complications. In the end, it was decided to use the affiliate libraries' existing nonprofit identification for funding applications rather than establish a separate 501(c)3 status for Health InfoNet.

The UAB Lister Hill Library to date has provided the primary organizational support for the service. Beyond training and collection development consultation, Lister Hill librarians also provide backup reference service for those health questions beyond the scope of the public libraries. The Lister Hill Library had an existing consumer health information service policy that was revised to reflect the new Health InfoNet setup. This includes question referral procedures instituted at the public librarians' request establishing forms for faxing questions to Lister Hill or for users to bring with them to the library.

Other library organizations expressed interest and support for the Health InfoNet project from its earliest days. The Alabama Health Libraries Association (ALHeLA) is a reliable champion, providing occasional financial as well as constant moral support and encouragement. The Jefferson County Reference Roundtable and the Alabama Public Library Service (APLS) have also endorsed the InfoNet service, providing opportunities for presentations about the project and training venues, as has the local chapter of the Special Libraries Association. Collaborative grant opportunities, mostly sponsored by the National Network of Libraries of Medicine, Southeastern Atlantic (NNLM/SE/A) region, opened up the way for other entities to become involved with Health InfoNet. Important partners in recent years include the Alabama State Health Planning and Development Agency (SHPDA), a government agency responsible for licensing health facilities; state and local public health agencies; and local church health ministries (see "Community Outreach" below). In the post–"Go Local" period (see "Health InfoNet Post–Go Local" below), there was an effort to identify partner health organizations to link to their online databases of services, thus (hopefully) reducing the labor needed to maintain the InfoNet database of health services on the site. The local United Way 2-1-1 service (http://www.211connectsalabama.org/search.aspx) was one such partner health organization. Others included the Alabama Lifespan Respite Resource Network (http://www.alabamarespite.org/), a state respite care organization, and other locally created online databases such as the Mental Health Resource Directory for Alabama (http://www.alabamamentalhealth.org/).

TRAINING

Training for public library staff in appropriate and effective health information services has always been an important function of the InfoNet program. The medical and public librarian partners directing Health InfoNet conduct regular workshops, which include:

- medical reference interviewing tips
- legal considerations, including differentiating between patient education and consumer health information
- weeding and collection development
- suggested resources, including the newly formed Alabama Virtual Library of licensed information resources for state residents
- background and procedures for Health InfoNet library participants

Onsite in-person workshops are still provided for public librarians, but increasingly the training is provided online, via synchronous or asynchronous methods. There is a self-paced tutorial for public library staff available on the Health InfoNet "Resources for Librarians" webpage (http://www.health infonet.org/Pages/Health-InfoNet-Resources-for-Librarians.aspx).

FUNDING

An ongoing concern for the InfoNet advisory panel and coordinators has been identifying funding opportunities to support the new service. The National Network of Libraries of Medicine's (NN/LM) outreach subcontract funding provided many opportunities over the years. During late 1999 a proposal, "Access to Electronic Health Information for the Public 1999," for approximately $40,000 was submitted to NN/LM. This proposal sought funding support not only for marketing, administration, and exhibit costs for Health InfoNet, but especially for personnel to overhaul the website. That personnel was a graduate library school student at the University of Alabama (Tuscaloosa), and the funding provided in 2000 and 2001 supported tuition costs and

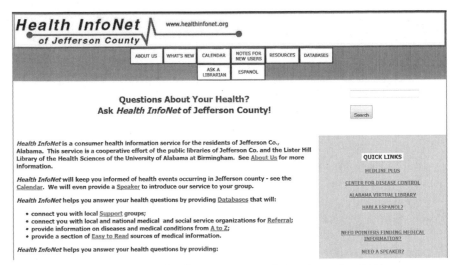

Figure 3.1. Health InfoNet of Jefferson County website, December 2001

a small stipend for her work on the site. The new site was unveiled in late 2001 (see figure 3.1). Improvements included not only a more professional look and easier navigability, but also features such as a section devoted to Spanish-language health information resources for the growing Latino community. (During this time a Spanish-language Health InfoNet brochure was also created.) Other sections on the website included standard policies such as linking guidelines and criteria for evaluating online health information.

The "Go Local" program was initiated by the National Library of Medicine (NLM) as a means to help health information users find relevant health services in their geographic location for their specific needs. The pilot project was conducted in North Carolina starting in 2001, and NLM used the lessons learned from that pilot to create centralized computer support for Go Local services databases in various locations as well as funding to support the initial creation of those databases (Olney, Backus, and Klein, 2010). Health InfoNet of Alabama, with the backing of APLS and a new partner, the State Health Planning and Development Agency (SHPDA), applied for the special funding opportunity to support hiring another graduate library student from the University of Alabama to prepare the expanded database of services to NLM's Go Local standards. The Alabama Go Local proposal, including seed funding, was approved in May of 2004, making Health InfoNet the sixth consumer health information project in the nation selected as a Go Local participant.

Although Health InfoNet was an NLM-supported Go Local participant in that NLM provided the server space and technical support for the website and database of health services, the preparation of the data and content remained a local responsibility for InfoNet project coordinators, as did maintenance of the site. In order to expand the local database of services already available on the site, SHPDA offered to download its database of licensed health facilities throughout the state for the new site. This offer was gratefully accepted, and the data were downloaded and prepared according to requirements established by both NLM and Health InfoNet advisory panels. With the subsequent hiring of a graduate library student as well as the input of numerous librarian volunteers around the state, the database of health services was expanded further. The new Go Local site went live in September of 2005.

If NLM support and technical assistance made some aspects of managing the site easier, it did not make it easier to maintain and update a database of some four thousand records, especially with limited staff devoted to its upkeep and an uncertain supply of volunteers from libraries around the state. As time went by, NLM became increasingly concerned with the integrity of the records in the local projects, including Alabama's because of the backlog of unaudited records. Many Go Local site administrators around the country expressed concern about the time demands involved in maintaining their sites as well as the limited funding available to support hiring additional staff. With the combination of these concerns along with changing Internet directory resources and declining usage statistics for the Go Local sites, NLM ultimately decided to discontinue the project in early 2010 (Klein, 2010).

NN/LM funding would continue as a mainstay for Health InfoNet programs and services for many years, although other funding opportunities occasionally arose as well. Identifying sources of grant funding for purchases such as promotional items and website improvements is a challenge as competition grows for limited funds.

COLLECTIONS

One of the primary goals of Health InfoNet is the creation of optimal health collections in participating public libraries. To that end, a list of recommended materials for health collections in public libraries—aka the "core list"—is updated by the UAB Lister Hill Library on a biannual basis (formerly annual) to the public libraries via the Health InfoNet program. The tools for this task include reviews, other lists of recommended materials and such, and marking certain titles as "essential." Total costs for "essential" titles are generally kept below $400 to $600. Consumer health magazine titles are also included among the recommendations. Early core lists included print and video materials, but video and DVD titles were eventually phased out and

URLs for suggested websites added. Print and electronic book and journal titles have remained on the list (Health InfoNet of Alabama, 2014).

Since the public libraries' budgets vary, adherence to the core list is voluntary, and the recommendations are treated as suggested purchases only. Some libraries have been able to obtain Library Services and Technology Act (LSTA) funding on occasion to support purchasing all the titles or those in a specific subject area. Other occasional funding sources for this purpose include local foundations or voluntary health organizations.

Since aging health collections are as much of a concern, if not more, than adding new titles, special emphasis is placed on training public librarians to weed their health collections to conform to the five-year rule of thumb for health resource retention. Since some still have reservations about providing health information services in their libraries, the point about weeding is often made in a legal protection context.

MARKETING

A recurring topic at any Health InfoNet advisory committee meeting throughout its history has been that of marketing the service to potential users. While funding for promotion is limited, it is recognized that without it there is little point in providing the service at all since usage will be minimal if users aren't aware of the service. Some of the NN/LM and other grant funding has been used to support promotion efforts, including a 2009 National Information Center on Health Services Research (NICHSR) award that helped fund billboards in the Birmingham area promoting both Health InfoNet and United Way's 2-1-1 service (see figure 3.2). However, when marketing funds are difficult to come by, the InfoNet administrators make use of in-kind services and free public relations venues wherever possible. For example, marketing professionals on the Health InfoNet Advisory Committee arrange opportunities for free consultations with PR companies, and graphics student interns update the InfoNet brochures and provide detailed marketing plans for the service. Other important word-of-mouth PR opportunities are provided by health fairs at churches, events such as health agency-sponsored runs, and the like. The Alabama Public Library Service helps distribute InfoNet brochures to public libraries throughout the state, thus addressing the need for librarians themselves to be aware of the service. However, it remains a daunting task to keep Health InfoNet in the range of vision for potential users (and even participating librarians) with so much competition for attention from an ever-increasing tide of information sources.

Figure 3.2. NICHSR-funded promotional billboard, located in Birmingham, Alabama, 2009

COMMUNITY OUTREACH

The focus group surveys conducted during formation of Health InfoNet revealed some opportunities for outreach. A particular population in need of information outreach was middle-aged and older African American men, who noted that they felt left behind somewhat by recent information technology advancements. When a new NN/LM funding opportunity for community outreach was announced in 2001/2002, the advisory panel agreed that Health InfoNet should prepare a proposal focused on partnering with local black churches to reach this population. Since the federal government had recently endorsed the involvement of faith-based institutions in funding proposals, this type of collaboration was seen as very timely. The Jefferson County Department of Health connected the Health InfoNet project leaders with key faith leaders in the community via a local organization called Congregations for Public Health (CPH). The plan as presented to the funders entailed purchasing desktop computers, printers, and fax machines and installing them in the four participating churches, training an onsite facilitator to assist congregation members and neighboring residents with locating reliable health information via the Health InfoNet and MedlinePlus websites, and presenting talks on health topics of interest at each church throughout the grant period. This was the first of the "Healthy Spirit" projects, followed by a number of other collaborative health information outreach projects with Health InfoNet and CPH as partners in subsequent years.

Other community outreach collaborations in the new century have involved Health InfoNet in projects including organizations such as UAB Medicine, UAB School of Public Health, Cahaba Valley Health Care, UAB Department of Preventive Medicine, Alabama Cooperative Extension System, UAB School of Education, Jefferson County Department of Health, UAB Department of Sociology, Jefferson County Place Matters, United Way, the Alabama AHECs, the Alabama Lifespan Respite Resource Network, and the State Health Planning and Development Agency.

HEALTH INFONET POST–GO LOCAL

With the announcement of NLM discontinuing support for the Go Local project in 2010, the Health InfoNet administrators and advisory panel had a decision to make about the database of health services, since that was the most labor-intensive service associated with the program. (The choice of whether or not to continue with the Health InfoNet project as a whole was never questioned.) At a special called meeting of the advisory committee on April 20, 2010, the committee considered three options, as follows:

1. Option 1: Eliminate the database of health services on the site.
2. Option 2: Continue to support and update the database of Alabama health services, with the cooperation of partners such as United Way 2-1-1 and other organizations with existing databases of health services targeted to certain clientele.
3. Option 3: Continue to support a stripped-down version of the Go Local database, with partnering library entities only.

The quality of online search engine retrievals for local health services was a key focus of discussion during the meeting. It was noted that, for example, a sample Google search of "medical transportation" with geographic keywords added yielded a considerable number of false hits such as airport limousine services. Considering the older adult key users of Health InfoNet and the fact that many were not highly educated, it was reasonable to assume that leaving them to their own devices online would not be serving them well. After much discussion of the pros and cons for each option, the committee agreed that Option 2 was preferable. It was felt that linking to others' online databases for certain types of services rather than expending staff time maintaining those records in the InfoNet database was a better way of working within the local staffing and funding limitations after separating from NLM, while still offering what was perceived as a very valuable service to state residents.

Another immediate issue, having decided to maintain the website with its database of health services, was that of creating a new site locally within the relatively short time frame established by NLM for transferring the records. Since it was made clear that no funding would be made available from either NLM or the regional medical library for this purpose, this was an immediate cost that had to be borne locally. The University of Alabama at Birmingham (UAB) stepped up to support the cost for this new site, and Health InfoNet "came home" to Alabama in the fall of 2010 with a newly redesigned website. (In 2014 the site was again redesigned to take advantage of responsive design technology to allow optimal site viewing on any computer or mobile device.)

Linking to other state-based health services databases did not lighten the Health InfoNet database maintenance load as much as the administrators had hoped. Furthermore, the institutional technical security measures at UAB created barriers for non-UAB database administrators in working on the database. In 2014, a graduate student assistant at UAB was hired part-time to audit and maintain the existing records, while the program administrators continued to add new records to the database.

ASSESSMENT

Regular evaluation of effectiveness is a requirement for any library service, and consumer health information services are no exception. Certainly grant funders will expect an assessment component as part of any funding proposal. The problem for Health InfoNet lies in the collaborative multi-institutional nature of its organization. Public libraries, which are already stretched by competing demands and limited budgets, are not generally open to creating separate accounting measures for health-related requests. So, other than the tallies for the Birmingham Public Libraries created during the initial grant-funding period of 2001, there are no data available on the extent of user demand for medical reference assistance in the public libraries in Alabama. The temporary tracking of health information requests by the forty-one participating public libraries during a sample period during pre-9/11, 2001 revealed an average of over one thousand health questions per month per library. This level of activity exists despite the earlier focus groups finding that libraries were relatively low on the list of places people thought of when they had health questions.

Likewise, the participating medical libraries have found it difficult to keep separate tallies of consumer health questions received. In addition, since the public libraries in Health InfoNet have not been enthusiastic about tracking such data, the medical libraries have less incentive to do so on their own.

If traditional user-request data have been unavailable, however, other measures of effectiveness have been tracked. As suggested by Olney and Barnes (2013), the "mixed method" approach using both quantitative and qualitative measures has been employed to try to get a complete picture of the health of Health InfoNet. Such methods include the following:

- surveys of librarians and advisory committee members
- website and social networking accounts analytics
- "process evaluations" such as numbers of InfoNet database records added/updated, or numbers of exhibits and presentations
- grant funding and reports
- workshop evaluations
- consumer information packet evaluations
- testimonials

Each individual method has its limitations. In particular, surveys suffer from a low response rate, even surveys of participating librarians. Online survey methods such as Survey Monkey (https://www.surveymonkey.com) have made it easier to design surveys and respond to them, but the evidentiary weight of survey results by themselves should be viewed skeptically. Still, within the limitations of the assessment methods available and the inherent problems within each method, the cumulative picture has provided a "good enough" overview of the effectiveness of this health information service.

So, how effective has Health InfoNet been judging by this mixed bag of assessment techniques? A long-term view would probably assign high grades in terms of outreach effectiveness, particularly in terms of relationship building among other nonprofit health agencies and information providers, including faith-based health ministries. A lesser grade might be assigned in terms of reach among the general population, mostly due to lack of marketing funds and competition for attention in the current information-rich environment. Certain high points, such as the core list of recommended health materials, have declined in popularity somewhat, while other initially less successful measures, such as the website design and usage, have improved over time. Since Health InfoNet is still a work in progress, the final judgment remains to be made.

The Health InfoNet of Alabama program is at a pivotal point in its existence, not only due to a transition in leadership currently under way, but also because of the changing landscape of health information in the second decade of the twenty-first century. The new strategic planning team that was formed in the summer of 2015 will look at every aspect of the service to determine what works, what doesn't, what might be improved, and what should be relinquished in response to current user needs and expectations. It will be an exciting time for Health InfoNet!

LESSONS LEARNED

As this brief history of Health InfoNet of Alabama has undoubtedly demonstrated, there have been a number of both successes and missteps during its creation and implementation. The following is a list of lessons learned by the project administrators.

Organization

- "Ready, Fire, Aim" vs. analysis paralysis: It's important to strike a balance between the absolute necessity of thoughtful planning in considering all aspects of initiating a consumer health information service and the need to act (or not). There should be a mix of personalities on the planning team, that is both cautious planners and gung-ho "doers." If they can work through their personality differences without killing each other, they may come up with the best plan possible.
- Formalize relationships among institutional partners from the beginning: A "memorandum of understanding," or MOU, may be advisable, specifying the expected roles and responsibilities of each partner, including financial support of the project.

Funding

- Budget for adequate funding: Ask administrators for appropriate funds for the project from the beginning. Neither they nor the project are well served by half-promises and wishful thinking about the low costs involved. This is not a cheap endeavor, not if it's done well.

Staffing

- Volunteers vs. staff: Volunteers are nice, but paid staff are better and more reliable. Estimate realistic personnel needs in initial planning and review those staffing needs regularly.
- Delegate tasks and accept help where offered: Project administrators should avoid the "Little Red Hen" syndrome. No one person can or should perform all the tasks associated with this type of project, regardless of its organization.

Community Outreach

- Recognize supporters: Be sure to recognize supporters, volunteers, advisory committee members, and other partners in whatever ways are available. Newsletter profiles of individuals or organizations are always nice—and inexpensive—ways to recognize people and agencies who have helped promote project goals, for example.

General

- Be opportunistic: Don't be afraid to take advantage of opportunities that may arise throughout the project lifetime! These opportunities may come in the form of funding availability, awards, partnerships, PR and media attention, and other support. This opportunism should be accompanied by an ability to be flexible enough to rearrange priorities if an important opportunity is time-limited, of course.
- Celebrate success: Be sure to have fun and celebrate milestones and successes along the way!

CONCLUSION

A good consumer health information service, however it is organized, is something to take pride in as a valuable community resource for people who may be at a low point in their lives. Keeping the end user in mind is what has guided Health InfoNet of Alabama throughout its history. Let this compass point—the users' needs—guide you as well!

REFERENCES

Health InfoNet of Alabama. 2011. *Questions About Your Health? We're Your Health Information Experts and We're in Your Neighborhood!* Unpublished brochure.

Health InfoNet of Alabama. 2014. "Recommended Core List of Books and Journals for Alabama Public Libraries." Healthinfonet of Alabama. http://www.healthinfo net.org/Documents/HealthInfoNetCore%20Listrev2014.pdf.

Klein, Lori J. 2010. "NLM to Discontinue Support of MedlinePlus Go Local." *NLM Technical Bulletin* no. 373 (March–April). National Library of Medicine. https:// www.nlm.nih.gov/pubs/techbull/ma10/ma10_go_local_discontinue.html.

Olney, Cynthia A., Joyce E. B. Backus, and Lori J. Klein. 2010. "Characteristics of Project Management at Institutions Sponsoring National Library of Medicine MedlinePlus Go Local." *Journal of the Medical Library Association* 98, no. 1 (January): 65–72.

Olney, Cynthia A., and Susan J. Barnes. 2013. *Collecting and Analyzing Evaluation Data*. 2nd ed. National Network of Libraries of Medicine. https://nnlm.gov/sites/default/files/migrated/file/f487b1664a1606a6b663b4dcfb65f0e8.pdf.

Rees, Alan M., ed. 1991. *Managing Consumer Health Information Services*. Phoenix, AZ: Oryx Press.

UAB (University of Alabama at Birmingham) Center for Health Promotion, Survey Research Unit. 2000. *Report of Health Information Needs/Library Use Focus Groups*. Unpublished report.

4

Consumer Health Information Service in the Public Library

BARBARA M. BIBEL, *Oakland Public Library*

The public library is a vital resource for people seeking health and medical information. It is a familiar community institution used to meet information needs in many areas (Deering and Harris, 1996). People are used to going to the library for recreational reading, public programs, and computer access, so seeking health information there is natural (Tyckoson, 2002).

Health and medical questions are among the most common queries at public library reference desks. Patients and family members seeking information about a disease or condition, students doing reports, and members of the public curious about the latest breakthrough touted in the news media turn to the library for help. With health care providers under serious time constraints, patients need to find information, and they often need guidance to locate it. The Internet is a major source, but finding accurate, current information that lay readers can understand may be difficult. Librarians can help, and people know that they are available and willing.

Librarians play an important role in promoting health awareness and health literacy by providing access to reliable resources on topics such as anatomy and physiology, diseases and conditions, nutrition, fitness, and drugs. They teach patrons how to use these sources so that they can find what they need and evaluate what they find in both print and online resources. It is not uncommon for people to ask whether a particular treatment or drug is the correct one or the best one for a particular condition. When that happens, a librarian can locate objective information and encourage the patron to discuss it with his or her health care practitioner. Informed patients who actively participate in their care have better outcomes (Ullrich and Vaccaro, 2002).

COMMUNITY ASSESSMENT

To provide quality health information service, public librarians need to do several things. First of all, they must learn about their communities. Gathering demographic information about the age, ethnicity, education, languages spoken, and literacy levels of the population will help them plan appropriate collection development and programming. The U.S. Bureau of the Census, state agencies, and school districts offer useful information in these areas. The U.S. Bureau of the Census website (http://www.census.gov) is a good starting point. The American FactFinder (http://factfinder.census.gov) and Easy Stats (http://www.census.gov/easystats) tools allow librarians to obtain community profiles at either a city, county, or census-tract level that is specific to the smaller community served by a branch library. A detailed community profile will include information about the ages, educational attainment, languages spoken, English-language ability, place of birth and citizenship, disability, gender, marital status, and grandparents raising grandchildren. School districts and community organizations also collect useful relevant data. The Robert Wood Johnson Foundation produces County Health Rankings & Roadmaps (http://www.countyhealthrankings.org), which profiles health and environmental issues within specific counties. These resources will help librarians learn about community health and social issues so that they can plan programs, select materials, conduct outreach, establish partnerships, and design classes that will benefit their communities. They will also be able to market their services effectively.

COLLECTION DEVELOPMENT

To provide good reference service, the library needs a strong collection of health and medical information. Ideally, a librarian with knowledge and interest in the subject should be in charge of the collection. It should include both print and electronic resources. It should also include materials in the languages spoken in the community as well as materials at a variety of reading levels. The Institute for Healthcare Advancement (http://www.iha4health.org) publishes the What to Do for Health series, which contains reasonably priced books on basic health care for adults, infants, teens, and seniors in English, Spanish, Chinese, Vietnamese, and Korean. These are written at the third- to fifth-grade reading level, so English-language learners and low-literacy patrons can use them easily.

The collection should include medical and allied health dictionaries, general medical encyclopedias, and reference books about drugs. Both reference and circulating materials about basic anatomy and physiology; diseases and conditions; prescription, nonprescription, and recreational drugs; complementary and alternative medicine; health insurance; and caregiving should be available. Patrons often want to find health care providers, so directories of local physicians, dentists, hospitals, and community organizations will be very useful. Subscriptions to lay health magazines and newsletters such as the *Harvard Health Letter*, *Consumer Reports Health*, and *MedlinePlus Magazine* as well as a few major medical journals such as *JAMA*, *New England Journal of Medicine*, and *Lancet* will provide both advice and access to major medical studies that find their way into headline news. Librarians should be aware that professional medical journals have a high readability level and that understanding clinical research is not easy (Baker and Wilson, 1996). Medical dictionaries and other sources that explain how to interpret clinical studies such as Greenhalgh's *How to Read a Paper* (2014) will help both patrons and librarians who use these journals. Videos are also popular because they provide information about common health problems as well as exercise programs. They are useful for patrons who have low literacy skills as well.

Computers for searching subscription databases and free health websites are a necessity for both patrons and staff. Gale Health Reference Center and EBSCO Consumer Health Complete both offer comprehensive coverage of health information at the lay level. Libraries that belong to a consortium can negotiate favorable prices for subscriptions. There is also a great deal of high-quality online information available at no cost from government agencies and nonprofit organizations. The National Library of Medicine's PubMed and MedlinePlus databases, the Centers for Disease Control and Prevention (CDC), and the American Diabetes Association are examples of free resources.

Selecting materials in other languages can be tricky. It is relatively easy to find materials in Spanish. Major distributors such as Baker and Taylor and Brodart have Spanish materials and staff specialists to assist librarians. Other languages are more difficult, but there are vendors. It is important to check the materials carefully because they may not be current. Publishers may sell translation rights for older editions. It is also difficult to find reviews of materials in other languages. MedlinePlus (http://medlineplus.gov) and Healthy Roads Media (http://www.healthyroadsmedia.org) provide health and medical information in a variety of languages that has been vetted by health professionals. Both of these resources are free. See appendix 1 for a list of vendors.

Selecting appropriate materials is vital. Medical and health information changes rapidly, so it is important to maintain a current collection. While books on anatomy and medical history have a longer shelf life, those about diseases and drug therapy should be weeded every three to five years. To find good current books, librarians may consult the reviews in *Booklist*, *Library Journal*, and *Consumer Connection*. *Consumer Connection* is published online by the Consumer and Patient Health Information Section of the Medical Library Association at http://www.caphis.mlanet.org. This website includes reviews of books written by consumer health librarians as well as a list of the top one hundred consumer health websites, core collection lists, and information about providing consumer health information services. *Reference Sources for Small and Medium-Sized Libraries*, 8th ed. (O'Gorman, 2014), published by the American Library Association, offers lists of recommended resources with annotations. It has chapters about health and medicine and psychology and psychiatry that will be helpful for librarians selecting materials. Paying close attention to the questions asked at the reference desk will be helpful because they offer clues to community information needs. Many questions about asthma or diabetes, for example, may indicate the prevalence of these conditions in a given area.

THE REFERENCE INTERVIEW

The reference interview is vital. It is where the librarian establishes a relationship with the patron and determines his or her information needs. It also provides an opportunity to assess language needs and literacy levels. Consumer health information is unique because, in many cases, it literally affects the patron's life. Someone who has been diagnosed with a serious illness or is seeking information on behalf of a friend or family member with a serious illness may be very upset. The patron may be uncomfortable discussing personal information and may not completely understand the diagnosis. He or she may have incomplete information or garbled/misspelled medical terminology. The librarian must patiently sort everything out before beginning to answer the question. Ideally, a private space for consultation would be available, but this is rare in public libraries. Taking the patron to a quiet corner or table may be helpful. Asking him or her to provide as much information as possible about the question, listening carefully, and repeating it back to be sure that the librarian understands will help in the selection of appropriate information. Patrons may have unreasonable expectations about what the library can provide. There may not be an easy answer to a complex question. The librarian cannot diagnose or recommend treatments. He or she can offer objective, evidence-based information so that the patron may make an informed decision.

Although personally coming into the library offers the best opportunity to provide a wide range of information, some patrons are unable to do so.

They may call on the telephone, e-mail, or use chat reference service. Librarians can provide quick, ready-reference answers by telephone, but complex questions that require more time and in-depth research will require a trip to the library and/or an offer to e-mail or send more information via the postal service. Chat reference offers an opportunity for a more detailed interview, but it requires sufficient staffing because it takes time. E-mail reference allows patrons who are unable to come to the library to obtain information, but it may require multiple transactions. A well-designed form on the library website will make it more efficient.

LEGAL AND ETHICAL CONSIDERATIONS

Librarians are information professionals, not health care professionals. They provide information, but they cannot diagnose, treat, or recommend therapies or health care providers. This may disappoint some patrons, but explaining the situation and encouraging them to discuss the information that they obtained with their practitioner is the appropriate response. Providing information is the responsibility of the librarian. This means that if, for any reason, a request cannot be fulfilled, the librarian must refer the patron to someone who can provide the information. If it is a source that is not available at the library, a nearby medical library may have it. If a librarian feels uncomfortable answering a question for personal reasons, he or she must ask a colleague to handle the transaction. Librarians must also protect patron privacy. Medical reference work often deals with intimate details, so assuring the patron that the information will not be shared is important. If the library maintains a reference log, list the question without any patron identification. Adhering to the Library Bill of Rights and the American Library Association and Medical Library Association Code of Ethics will assure that patrons will receive high-quality information. See appendices 2, 3, and 4 for these documents.

TRAINING

Training is vital for providing good consumer health reference service. The National Library of Medicine began a pilot program to "learn about the role of public libraries in providing health information" in 1998 (Wood et al., 2000: 314). The Public Library Association began to promote collaboration between public libraries, community organizations, and medical libraries as well (Calvano and Needham, 1996). Training is an integral part of both of these projects. In 2001, the National Library of Medicine presented a preconference at the American Library Association midwinter conference in Washington, D.C. It offered basic tools for public librarians. The Medical Library Association (MLA) followed this with the unveiling of its Consumer Health Information Specialist program, which provides classes leading to certification. Librarians must take twelve hours of MLA-approved training to qualify at the basic level and twenty-four hours for certification at Level II. Certification must be renewed every three years by taking eight hours of continuing education. Public librarians can use this as an opportunity to develop their medical reference skills.

The National Network of Libraries of Medicine (NN/LM) offers free training through its Regional Medical Libraries (RMLs). These free classes are offered both in person and online. The schedules are available on their website (http://nnlm.gov). NN/LM also has many other tools available on its website: tutorials, training documents, information about grants, and staff available for consultation and on-site training. Public libraries may join NN/LM as affiliate members.

MLA also offers training at both its national and regional conferences. It is not free, but public librarians are welcome to attend. The Consumer and Patient Health Information Section (CAPHIS) has a great deal of useful information at http://www.caphis.mlanet.org: a newsletter, information about the Consumer Health Information Specialist program, a newsletter with book reviews, and detailed plans for running a consumer health information program. Other useful resources for training include Webjunction (https://webjunction.org), which offers free training on many library topics, including health, and Infopeople (http://www.infopeople.org). Infopeople training is for California librarians, but its webinars are archived and available to all on the website. They cover a wide range of topics.

Public librarians must also provide training for patrons and staff. Staff need to know how to locate and evaluate health and medical information. They in turn will assist the public with their searches. Since public libraries are a major source of computer access for many people, offering training in both basic Internet use and finding and evaluating health information is an important community service. Librarians can also educate users who contact them via e-mail or chat reference. By providing links to current, reliable websites and explaining what to look for when searching, librarians will help patrons improve their health literacy skills.

OUTREACH

Public libraries are a trusted community resource. By going out into the community, librarians can introduce people to their resources and learn more about their information needs. Attending community meetings, going to schools, and participating in local fairs increases the library's visibility. Hosting a health fair at the library will bring many people in. It offers an opportunity for people to get health screening and information about community services as well as a chance for librarians to introduce relevant resources. Having enrollment counselors in the library during open enrollment periods for Medicare and Affordable Care Act coverage is another excellent opportunity to provide useful service and increase visibility.

COLLABORATION AND PARTNERSHIP

Collaboration helps both public and medical librarians. Joint training efforts are very useful. Medical librarians can educate public librarians about various health topics and suggest resources to fill gaps in their collections. Public librarians can educate medical librarians about the information needs of the community and about working with a wide range of patrons. When public libraries partner with local hospital or academic medical libraries, both parties gain. Oakland Public Library (OPL) in California has a long-standing partnership with both the Health Education Center and the Health Sciences Library at Kaiser Permanente Medical Center in Oakland, California. The librarian, a recently retired consumer health information specialist certified by MLA, and the health sciences librarian at Kaiser share resources and refer patrons to one another. They also teach quarterly classes about health information to both the OPL staff and the public. This joint training and outreach increases the visibility of both institutions and provides the public with valuable health information. The librarians teach classes for local library staff on searching MedlinePlus and PubMed and about health resources on specific topics such as nutrition and women's health. The classes have been well received and librarians from the Greater Bay Area send staff to them. Classes for the public about finding and evaluating health information online and health information for travelers are also popular. Kaiser's Health Education Center also donated a collection of videos to OPL on common health topics in English, Spanish, and Chinese. The librarian has assisted the Health Education Center with collection development since they do not have a librarian. These efforts increase the competency of the staff and foster respect for both institutions in the community.

Working with other staff members within the library to promote health information is also very effective. OPL has a popular series of programs about travel featuring authors of the Lonely Planet Guides and other local adventurers. Lonely Planet is based in Oakland, so the publisher is happy to participate. Working with her colleague who developed the program, the librarian was able to add a session about health information for travelers to the series. She later presented a program about medical tourism to a very interested audience. Attendees at both programs learned about the resources available from the CDC, the Department of State, and the National Library of Medicine that will help them plan healthy journeys.

Libraries with adult literacy and teen programs offer further opportunities for collaboration. Incorporating health literacy skills and creating appropriate instructional materials are important activities for consumer health librarians. Creating programs for these groups will bring more people to the library and provide much needed education for groups that are often overlooked.

BEST PRACTICES

- Know your community so that you can provide the best services. Familiarity with the demographics, languages spoken, and literacy levels will ensure appropriate collection development choices. It will also guide programming.
- Take advantage of the resources available from the National Library of Medicine through your Regional Medical Library. The classes, materials, and staff support will offer opportunities for training and improve the level of consumer health information service.
- Train your staff so that all of them can provide quality medical reference service. High-quality service will improve the health of the community and increase awareness of the library as a trusted neighborhood resource.

CONCLUSION

Public libraries play a vital role in providing health information and promoting health literacy. Since the majority of public library systems in the United States are in rural areas, they may be the only source of health information available to many people (Gillaspy, 2005). By providing print and electronic resources, Internet access, and training for the public, librarians promote health awareness and increase the level of health literacy in their communities. This is important for everyone, but it is especially important for senior citizens because they often face more health challenges. Those who do not have sufficient information to understand their diagnosis and treatment plans have more hospitalizations, longer hospital stays, more physician visits, and more medication and treatment errors. They often lack the necessary skills for navigating the health care system effectively (National Academy on Aging

Society, 1999). When public libraries partner with medical libraries in the task of providing information, the result will be better health for their communities. Informed patients have better outcomes because they understand their conditions and participate as full partners in their care (Donohue, 2001). Librarians facilitate this process by providing the necessary tools.

APPENDIX 1: RESOURCES FOR MATERIALS IN OTHER LANGUAGES

Book Dealers and Distributors

Asian Languages

Eastwind Books, 1435 Stockton St., San Francisco, CA 94133. 415-772-5888. www.eastwindbooks.com. Publications from Hong Kong and China.

Kingstone Books, 3288 Pierce Street, Suite 190, Richmond, CA 94804. 510-527-6856. Publications from Taiwan.

Kinokuniya Books, 1581 Webster St., San Francisco, CA 94115. 415-567-6787. www.kinokuniya.com. Publications in Japanese and Chinese.

Pan Asian Publications, 29564 Union City Blvd. Union City, CA 94587. 510-475-1185. http://www.panap.com. Chinese, Hmong, Khmer, Korean, Tagalog, Thai, Vietnamese. Has bilingual books. Adult and juvenile.

San Jose Christian Books/Seoul Books, 1082 E. El Camino Real #5, Sunnyvale, CA 94087. 408-246-2300. Publications in Korean.

Farsi/Persian

Ketab, 1419 Westwood Blvd., Los Angeles, CA 90024. 310-477-7477. ketab1@ketab.com. http://www.ketab.com. Books, audio, video. Adult and Juvenile.

Raha Books, 441 La Prenda Rd., Los Altos, CA 94024. 650-947-7242. info@rahabooks.com. Publications in Farsi—audio, video, periodicals, books. Adult and Juvenile.

French

Amazon France, http://www.amazon.fr. Site is in French.

French Books Online, 11882 W. Stanford Place, Morrison, CO 80465. 303-993-6488. info@frenchbooksonline.com. http://www.frenchbooksonline.com.

Librarie Internationale Touzot, 62 Avenue de Suffren, Paris 75015 France 01 45 67 18 38. jtouzot@touzot.fr. http://www.touzot.fr. Bookstore 38 rue Saint-Sulpice Paris 75006 France 33 1 43 26 03 88.

Spanish

Baker & Taylor, 2550 West Tyvola Rd., Suite 300, Charlotte, NC 28217. 800-775-1700. btinfo@btol.com. www.btol.com.

Bilingual Publications, 270 Lafayette St., New York, NY 10012-3327. 212-431-3500. Has Facebook page.

Brodart, 500 Arch St., Williamsport, PA 17701. 800-474-9816. http://www.brodart.com. Nerissa Moran, Spanish-language specialist 1-800-233-8467 ext. (7) 6279. nmoran@brodart.com.

Lectorum, 205 Chubb Ave., Lyndhurst, NJ 07071. lectorum@lectorum.com. http://www.lectorum.com.

Tomo Books, P.O. Box 14052, Fresno, CA 93650. 559-836-7589, 559-289-2367. tomobooksusa@gmail.com.

Russian

Mikhail Freydlin, 56-20 212 St., Bayside, NY 11364. 347-987-4718. mif bookclub@yahoo.com. http://www.russieknigi.com.

Multicultural Books and Videos, 30007 John R Road, Madison Heights, MI 48071. 248-559-2676. 800-567-2220. service@multiculturalbv.com. www.multiculturalbooksandvideos.com. Arabic, Chinese, Farsi/Persian, French, German, Italian, Korean, Portuguese, Russian, Spanish, Tagalog, Vietnamese, Bengali, Gujarati, Hindi, Kannada, Malaysian, Punjabi, Tamil, Japanese, Polish, Somali, Croatian, Romanian, Turkish, Haitian-Creole, Amharic. Adult and Juvenile.

Russia Online, Inc., 10335 Kensington Parkway, Kensington, MD 20895. 301-933-0607. books@russia-on-line.com. http://www.russia-on-line.com. Also has Albanian, Czech, French, Latvian, Polish, Romanian, Serbian, Spanish, Ukranian.

Russian House Bookstore, 235 Fifth Avenue, New York, NY 10016. 212-685-1010. Multi-language

Book Fairs

Barcelona Liber Barcelona. Every two years. Usually in October.

Book Expo America (BEA). Annual in New York. Usually in May. http://www.bookexpoamerica.com. Large trade show with many publishers. *Library Journal* sponsors events for librarians at the fair.

Frankfurt. Frankfurt Book Fair. Annual. Usually in October.

Guadalajara Feria Internacional del Libro. http://www.fil.com.mx. Annual, end of November/early December. ALA provides some sponsorship for U.S. librarians. Great for Spanish-language materials.

Hong Kong Book Fair. Annual, usually in July. http://hkbookfair.hktdc.com/en/.

Jerusalem. Every two years, in odd years. Usually in February.

Taiwan Book Fair Taipei International Book Fair. Annual, in January. http://www.tibe.org.tw/new/index.php?lan=en.

Websites

DeafMD. http://www.deafmd.org. Provides information about common health problems in American Sign Language and has a directory of deaf-friendly physicians.

Ethnomed. http://www.ethnomed.org. Has information about various cultures and cross-cultural health as well as patient education materials in several languages.

Health Canada. http://www.hc-sc.gc.ca/hc-ps/index-eng.php. Has information in English and French.

Health Information Translations. http://www.healthinformationtranslations.com. Has information from Ohio medical institutions on disaster preparedness, diagnostic tests, fitness, and diseases in many languages.

Health Services Research Information Central. http://www.nlm.nih.gov/hsrinfo/disparities.html. Provides information about health and healthcare disparities as well as toolkits for outreach to various communities.

Healthy Roads Media. http://www.healthyroadsmedia.org. Material in many languages—written, audio, and streaming video. Has mobile app.

MedlinePlus. http://medlinplus.gov. Information in many languages. Has mobile version.

National Network of Libraries of Medicine. http://www.nnlm.nlm.nih.gov. Has a variety of information and tools for providing consumer health information, including a list of resources for multilingual materials.

Refugee Health Information Network. http://www.rhin.org. Has multilingual health information for refugees.

Special Information Services of the U.S. Department of Health and Human Services. http://www.sis.nlm.nih.gov/outreach.html. Has information about specific communities and multicultural resources.

SPIRAL: Selected Patient Information Resources in Asian Languages. http://www.library.tufts.edu/hsl/spiral/. Has consumer health information in Chinese, Hmong, Khmer, Korean, Laotian, Thai, and Vietnamese.

APPENDIX 2: THE LIBRARY BILL OF RIGHTS

The American Library Association affirms that all libraries are forums for information and ideas, and that the following basic policies should guide their services.

I.   Books and other library resources should be provided for the interest, information, and enlightenment of all people of the community the library serves. Materials should not be excluded because of the origin, background, or views of those contributing to their creation.

II. Libraries should provide materials and information presenting all points of view on current and historical issues. Materials should not be proscribed or removed because of partisan or doctrinal disapproval.

III. Libraries should challenge censorship in the fulfillment of their responsibility to provide information and enlightenment.

IV. Libraries should cooperate with all persons and groups concerned with resisting abridgment of free expression and free access to ideas.

V.   A person's right to use a library should not be denied or abridged because of origin, age, background, or views.

VI. Libraries which make exhibit spaces and meeting rooms available to the public they serve should make such facilities available on an equitable basis, regardless of the beliefs or affiliations of individuals or groups requesting their use.

Source: http://www.ala.org/advocacy/intfreedom/librarybill/
Adopted June 19, 1939. Amended October 14, 1944; June 18, 1948; February 2, 1961; June 27, 1967; and January 23, 1980; inclusion of "age" reaffirmed January 23, 1996, by the ALA Council. Used with the permission of the American Library Association.

APPENDIX 3: CODE OF ETHICS OF
THE AMERICAN LIBRARY ASSOCIATION

As members of the American Library Association, we recognize the importance of codifying and making known to the profession and to the general public the ethical principles that guide the work of librarians, other professionals providing information services, library trustees and library staffs. Ethical dilemmas occur when values are in conflict. The American Library Association Code of Ethics states the values to which we are committed, and embodies the ethical responsibilities of the profession in this changing information environment. We significantly influence or control the selection, organization, preservation, and dissemination of information. In a political system grounded in an informed citizenry, we are members of a profession explicitly committed to intellectual freedom and the freedom of access to information. We have a special obligation to ensure the free flow of information and ideas to present and future generations. The principles of this Code are expressed in broad statements to guide ethical decision making. These statements provide a framework; they cannot and do not dictate conduct to cover particular situations.

I.   We provide the highest level of service to all library users through appropriate and usefully organized resources; equitable service policies; equitable access; and accurate, unbiased, and courteous responses to all requests.

II.   We uphold the principles of intellectual freedom and resist all efforts to censor library resources.

III.   We protect each library user's right to privacy and confidentiality with respect to information sought or received and resources consulted, borrowed, acquired or transmitted.

IV.   We respect intellectual property rights and advocate balance between the interests of information users and rights holders.

V.   We treat coworkers and other colleagues with respect, fairness, and good faith, and advocate conditions of employment that safeguard the rights and welfare of all employees of our institutions.

VI.   We do not advance private interests at the expense of library users, colleagues, or our employing institutions.

VII.   We distinguish between our personal convictions and professional duties and do not allow our personal beliefs to interfere with fair representation of the aims of our institutions or the provision of access to their information resources.

VIII.   We strive for excellence in the profession by maintaining and enhancing our own knowledge and skills, by encouraging the professional development of coworkers, and by fostering the aspirations of potential members of the profession.

Adopted at the 1939 Midwinter Meeting by the ALA Council; amended June 30, 1981; June 28, 1995; and January 22, 2008.

Source: http://www.ala.org/advocacy/sites/ala.org.advocacy/files/content/proethics/codeofethics/Code%20of%20Ethics%20of%20the%20American%20Library%20Association.pdf. Used with the permission of the American Library Association.

APPENDIX 4: CODE OF ETHICS FOR HEALTH SCIENCES LIBRARIANSHIP (JUNE 2010–)

Goals and Principles for Ethical Conduct

The health sciences librarian believes that knowledge is the sine qua non of informed decisions in health care, education, and research, and the health sciences librarian serves society, clients, and the institution by working to ensure that informed decisions can be made. The principles of this code are expressed in broad statements to guide ethical decision making. These statements provide a framework; they cannot and do not dictate conduct to cover particular situations.

Society

- The health sciences librarian promotes access to health information for all and creates and maintains conditions of freedom of inquiry, thought, and expression that facilitate informed health care decisions.

Clients

- The health sciences librarian works without prejudice to meet the client's information needs.
- The health sciences librarian respects the privacy of clients and protects the confidentiality of the client relationship.
- The health sciences librarian ensures that the best available information is provided to the client.

Institution

- The health sciences librarian provides leadership and expertise in the design, development, and ethical management of knowledge-based information systems that meet the information needs and obligations of the institution.

Profession

- The health sciences librarian advances and upholds the philosophy and ideals of the profession.
- The health sciences librarian advocates and advances the knowledge and standards of the profession.
- The health sciences librarian conducts all professional relationships with courtesy and respect.
- The health sciences librarian maintains high standards of professional integrity.

Self

- The health sciences librarian assumes personal responsibility for developing and maintaining professional excellence.

• The health sciences librarian shall be alert to and adhere to his or her institution's code of ethics and its conflict of interest, disclosure, and gift policies.

Source: https://www.mlanet.org/about/ethics.html. Used with the permission of the Medical Library Association.

REFERENCES

Baker, Lynda M., and Feleta L. Wilson. 1996. "Consumer Health Materials Recommended for Public Libraries? Too Tough to Read?" *Public Libraries* 35, no. 2 (March/April): 124–130.

Calvano, Margaret, and George Needham. 1996. "Public Empowerment through Accessible Health Information." *Bulletin of the Medical Library Association* 84, no. 2 (April): 253–56.

Deering, Mary Jo, and John Harris. 1996. "Consumer Health Information Demand and Delivery: Implications for Libraries." *Bulletin of the Medical Library Association* 84, no. 2 (April): 209–16.

Donohue, Maureen. 2001. "Patient Education Holds the Key to Better Compliance Outcomes." *Family Practice News* (February 15). http://findarticles.com/p/articles/mi-m0BJI/is-4-31?pnum=28&opg=71900964.

Gillaspy, Mary L. 2005. "Factors Affecting the Provision of Consumer Health Information in Public Libraries: The Last Five years." *Library Trends* 53, no. 3 (Winter): 480–95.

Greenhalgh, Trisha. 2014. *How to Read a Paper: The Basics of Evidence-Based Medicine.* 5th ed. London: BMJ.

National Academy on Aging Society. 1999. Fact Sheet. "Low Health Literacy Skills Increase Health Care Expenditures by $73 Billion." http://www.agingsociety.org/agingsociety/publications/fact/fact_low.html.

O'Gorman, Jack, ed. 2014. *Reference Sources for Small and Medium-Sized Libraries.* 8th ed. Chicago: American Library Association.

Tyckoson, David. 2002. "On the Desirableness of Personal Relations between Librarians and Readers: The Past and Future of Reference Services." RUSA Forum. http://findarticles.com/p/articles/mi-m0BJI/is-4-31?pnum=2&opg+71900964.

Ullrich, Peter F. Jr., and Alexander R. Vaccaro. 2002. "Patient Education on the Internet: Opportunities and Pitfalls." *Spine* 27, no. 7 (April): 185–88.

Wood, Fred B., Becky Lyon, Mary Beth Snell, Paula Kitendaugh, Victor H. Cid, and Elliot R. Siegel. 2000. "Public Library Consumer Health Information Pilot Project: Results of a National Library of Medicine Evaluation." *Bulletin of the Medical Library Association* 88, no. 4 (October): 314–22.

5

Rewards and Challenges of Children's Health Education

An Ongoing Community Partnership to Reach Local Preschoolers

DEIDRA WOODSON AND DONNA F. TIMM,
LSU Health Shreveport Health Sciences Library

The LSU Health Shreveport Health Sciences Library faculty developed a successful and ongoing project to emphasize wellness issues for preschoolers in a creative manner. To accomplish this, the librarians offered health-related story times with follow-up activities at locations within the community. This chapter describes the specifics on how the librarians used stories and activities to capture the children's attention on wellness issues and to make those issues both fun and educational.

GOALS AND OBJECTIVES

When the library faculty embarked upon writing an outreach proposal in 2009, the librarians focused their efforts on health-related programs for children, a project that continues to this day. The library faculty had never before offered programming for children and thought that one way to reach them would be to plan story times on health-related issues such as exercise, nutrition, and heart health.

The overall goals of the project were as follows:

- Educate children about healthy habits through stories and activities.
- Create a web portal where children can access authoritative and free health information and games.
- Develop educational materials to support the health-related activities.
- Promote the health-related stories and activities through the web portal.

After setting the goals and objectives, the library faculty collaborated with a number of public libraries as well as Sci-Port, Louisiana's Science Center, to reach the target population of preschool and early elementary-aged children in low-income communities in Caddo Parish, Louisiana.

BACKGROUND

Over the past several decades, the number of adults and children who have become overweight or obese has increased worldwide at an alarming rate (Ng et al., 2014). Over one-third of adults and 17 percent of children are categorized as being obese, while 8 percent of children are classified as severely and morbidly obese (Ogden et al., 2014; Skinner and Skelton 2014). Research has demonstrated that obese children are four to six times more likely to be obese in adulthood than children with a normal weight (Serdula et al., 1993). Furthermore, children who struggle with being overweight or obese are much more susceptible to certain health conditions, such as dyslipidemia, hypertension, type 2 diabetes, non-alcoholic fatty liver disease, obstructive sleep apnea, lower-limb malalignment, and depression (Daniels, 2006; Gurnani, Birken, and Hamilton, 2015; Han, Lawlor, and Kimm, 2010).

Prevention is the preferred approach among the medical community to reverse the rate of obesity prevalence (Han, Lawlor, and Kimm, 2010). Numerous studies have been conducted testing the effectiveness of school-based obesity prevention programs, and most of the methods include education on nutrition, physical activity, sedentary behavior, or a combination of these (Amini et al., 2015; Safron et al., 2011). Studies also show that weight gain in preschool children is a significant predictor for obesity later in life (Brown et al., 2015; Hughes et al., 2014). Furthermore, obesity prevalence is higher in children from low-income families and minority children (Kumanyika and Grier, 2006). Therefore, the LSU Health Shreveport librarians decided to develop a children's health program designed for preschool and early elementary children from a low socioeconomic status to educate them about maintaining a healthy lifestyle.

PROGRAM DESCRIPTION

Funding

The National Network of Libraries of Medicine South Central Region (NN/ LM SCR) offers an Outreach Cooperative Agreement, formerly known as a subcontract, to the Resource Libraries within the region every year. Each year, LSU Health Shreveport librarians write a proposal for this agreement to develop an outreach program that focuses on either a particular population or subject area. In early 2009, library faculty proposed the children's health program, which was funded for a one-year period beginning on May 1, 2009, and ending on April 30, 2010. Due to the success of this project, the librarians proposed to expand the program the following year, and it was funded again for the 2010–2011 award year. After two years, the librarians decided to target a different population for the 2011–2012 period. However, the partners continued to request story times, so the librarians continued the program as a smaller portion of the overall award project. Even though the librarians have explored different projects for each subsequent award year, they continually maintain and update the children's health program as a smaller segment of each cooperative agreement.

The funding allotted to the program has covered the cost of purchasing books for the story hours, as well as the printing of promotional bookmarks. The cost of printing educational handouts, like color sheets, is also covered.

Web Portal

Previously, library faculty had created the consumer health web portal healthelinks (http://www.healthelinks.org), which links to National Library of Medicine (NLM) online resources like MedlinePlus (http://www.medlineplus.gov), as well as other authoritative websites. For this project, the librarians developed the For Kids section of healthelinks (http://healthelinks.org/kidshealth/), which connects to consumer health web resources designed for children. All resources were chosen based on the previously established selection criteria for healthelinks: authority, audience, disclosure, unbiased objectivity, currency, and design (LSU Health Shreveport Health Sciences Library, 2015). The site also is used to promote upcoming story times and provides a list of health-related online games.

Library faculty developed a specialized method for selecting educational games for inclusion on the For Kids site (Woodson, Jones, and Timm, 2012). After searching the Internet for potential games, they rated each resource based on the level of difficulty, educational value, authoritativeness, and presence of advertisements. The games awarded the highest number of points were then evaluated for reading level using the Flesch-Kincaid Grade Level and Flesch Reading Ease tests. The games with the highest scores and appropriate reading level were added to the site.

Partners

Partnerships within the community are essential for programs designed to involve members of that local community. For this project, the most logical partners were the children's librarians at the local public library system, the Shreve Memorial Library. The first year of the program, the librarians worked with three local branches. Two of the three libraries had well-established programs, in which young children and their teachers from nearby preschool and early elementary school classes attended every week. Attendance at the story hours at these branches averaged fifty to one hundred students. Unfortunately, the third branch had not established relationships with local schools, so only a few children attended.

For the second award year, the librarians partnered with two additional branches, as well as the local children's science museum, Sci-Port, Louisiana's Science Center. The museum would host hands-on educational programs for local school children, including special needs children. At Sci-Port, LSU Health Shreveport librarians still read stories, just as they did at the public library, but they developed different activities that were more hands-on and thus more suitable for smaller groups in the museum setting.

Once the main objectives of the outreach projects no longer focused on educating young children, the librarians continued to maintain these relationships, especially with the children's librarians at the public library branches with well-established children's programs. They asked for continued visits to their branches, so the LSU Health Shreveport librarians seized the opportunity to maintain these partnerships by continuing the program. Furthermore, the librarians continue to seek opportunities to partner with children's librarians at other branches within the community.

Stories and Activities

As with any ongoing project, the story time programs have evolved over the years. Initially, only one story was read, which was followed by a fun, yet educational, activity to reinforce the lessons learned from the story. However, after several story times, the librarians realized that reading one story did not take enough time, and the entire program was only fifteen to twenty minutes. Since the allotted time for story hours ranged from thirty minutes to an hour at the various branches, the librarians decided to include more stories for each event.

LSU Health Shreveport librarians selected the stories based on health-related content and the intended age of the audience. Unfortunately, a few of the original stories chosen were found to be too didactic, as the children seemed to lose interest in the stories. As the librarians gained experience with conducting these events, these books were replaced with more interesting stories. Also, most of the children attending the story times were African American. The librarians noticed that many of the health-related stories that they were reading featured Caucasian characters. Therefore, they began to actively search for books with more diverse characters, so that the children could more easily identify with the stories.

The first story hour conducted did not have a specific focus, other than to provide general instruction on maintaining a healthy lifestyle and preventing obesity. As the project progressed, story times were developed with more specific themes, namely nutrition, exercise, and hygiene. Although the librarians initially wanted to create educational programs to prevent obesity, they realized that other health topics would be worthwhile to pursue, as well. Hand hygiene was the first additional subject area developed, since educational programs are needed to prevent the spread of infections among young children (Guinan, McGuckin, and Ali, 2002). Eventually, the program was expanded to include even more themes, including heart health, sun safety, sleep habits, and dental health. These themed story hours were usually paired with the corresponding awareness month or a holiday. For example, the heart health story time is conducted every February to celebrate American Heart Month, and a nutrition-themed story hour is sometimes held in October to stress to children not to eat too much candy during Halloween.

The appendix includes a list of recommended book titles for health-related story times designed for preschool and early elementary school children. Descriptions of the activities developed for the story hours are listed below.

Nutrition

Library faculty developed the Grocery Bag game to teach children to distinguish between healthy and unhealthy foods. The children were taken on an imaginary adventure to the grocery store, and they were shown cards with pictures of different types of food. If the food featured on the card was healthy, then the children gave a "thumbs up" and cheered, and the card was placed in the bag. However, if the food was not healthy, then the children turned their thumbs down and booed, and the card was set aside as if being set back on the shelf at the grocery store (see figure 5.1). After conducting the activity at several different branches, the librarians decided to update the game to incorporate physical activity. Instead of simply cheering, the children would run in place when shown healthy food because it gives you energy. Rather than booing at unhealthy food, the children would move slowly because these foods cause sluggishness. All of the cards were easily made using Microsoft ClipArt images.

This game was adapted for the Collaborative Summer Library Program (http://www.cslpreads.org/) 2013 theme, "Dig into Reading." New cards featuring healthy foods grown in a garden and unhealthy foods were created

Figure 5.1.   Children boo at a cupcake during the Grocery Bag game (© 2010, Donna F. Timm)

and attached to wooden skewers. Next, packing foam was placed inside a shallow cardboard box. In this game, the healthy food cards were placed in the garden box, and the unhealthy food cards were set aside (see figure 5.2). This activity was combined with a project designed by the children's librarian at the Shreve Memorial Library Wallette Branch. She gave each child a cup of dirt and passed around a variety of vegetable seeds. With the help of their teachers, the children planted the seeds in the dirt. Then, they took the cups back to their schools, so that they could see firsthand how healthy foods are grown and harvested.

Exercise

Instead of conducting a boring exercise routine, library faculty developed an innovative activity involving imaginary sports. The children were taken rock climbing, in which they stretched their arms and legs. They played baseball by swinging an imaginary bat and running the bases in place. They played jump rope by simply jumping in place, and they even went swimming, in which they stretched their arms. Additionally, the children danced to the

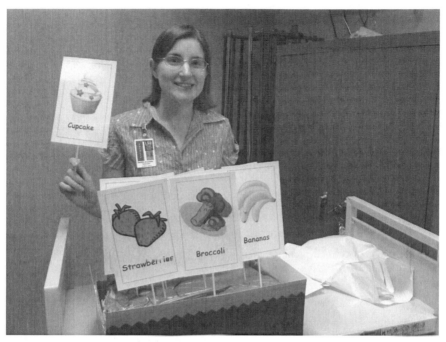

Figure 5.2.   Deidra Woodson poses with the Healthy Garden game (© 2013, Donna F. Timm)

Alvin and the Chipmunks' version of "The Twist" (1999). This activity has been conducted at numerous locations, including Sci-Port. Not only are the exercises fun for everyone, they are also easy to do in any setting. Also, children love to dance, so playing lively music to which they can move without realizing that they are exercising is highly recommended.

Heart Health

Every February, to celebrate American Heart Month, the librarians conduct a heart health-themed story hour at one or more of the Shreve Memorial Library branches. Librarians adapted the Heart Smart game created by the Department of Exercise and Sport Science at East Carolina University (Mahar et al., 2015). In this activity, children learn to distinguish between healthy and unhealthy habits and about the basic functions of the heart. Library faculty began by talking about the location and functions of the heart. Then, the children were shown cards, developed using Microsoft ClipArt, that represented a particular activity, such as "Eating Vegetables," "Eating a Hamburger with Fries," "Jumping Rope," and "Watching TV." If the activity was good for the heart, the kids jumped, but if the activity was bad for the heart, the kids squatted.

After discovering the book *Hear Your Heart* (listed in the appendix), library faculty had the idea to develop a craft project, in which the children made their own stethoscopes. The librarians created a coloring sheet with images of the heart obtained from Microsoft ClipArt and the words, "I can hear my heart with my stethoscope." The children were given these coloring sheets along with cardboard paper towel tubes. They were instructed to color the sheet and then wrap it around the tube and secure it with tape.

Hand Hygiene

Unfortunately, the public library settings were not ideal for a hand-washing exercise, mainly due to the number of children in attendance but also because the only sinks available were located in the public restrooms. Therefore, the librarians decided to give each child a small amount of hand sanitizer to teach hygiene. However, this activity was still a bit inconvenient because of the number of children. As a result, the medical librarians created another game to teach proper hygiene. They developed the Soapy/Germy Says activity, which is a different version of Simon Says. In this game, the children followed Soapy's instructions, by mimicking actions like "wash your hands." However, when Germy gives instructions like "sneeze on your friends," the children told Germy "no."

Also, a number of hand-washing songs are available online to ensure that children wash their hands for the recommended length of time. At first, the librarians chose one of these freely available songs to teach the children, but after conducting numerous hand hygiene story times, they developed their own special song, which is included in the textbox.

I'M GONNA WASH THOSE GERMS RIGHT OFF OF MY HANDS

(Sung to the tune of "I'm Gonna Wash That Man Right Out of My Hair" from *South Pacific*)

I'm gonna wash those germs right off of my hands,
I'm gonna wash those germs right off of my hands,
I'm gonna wash those germs right off of my hands,
And send them down the drain.

I'm gonna rub and scrub with soap and water,
I'm gonna rub and scrub with soap and water,
I'm gonna rub and scrub with soap and water,
Now, rinse them down the drain.

Bye, Bye, Germs!

A different activity was conducted at Sci-Port, since the children's museum allowed for more hands-on activities. The children were given lotion to rub on their hands and were then instructed to place their hands in a bowl filled with green glitter. The glitter represented germs, and the children had to wash their hands until every speck of glitter was gone. This activity was simple to conduct and provided a visual representation of microorganisms to teach them how to effectively wash their hands.

Sun Safety

As part of the summer reading opening programs at several of the Shreve Memorial Library branches, the librarians conducted sun safety activities. They modified the "Sunny Says" activity from the SunWise program created by the Environmental Protection Agency (2014). In this game, which follows the format of Simon Says, the children respond to Sunny's directions like "put your hat on" and ignore the non-Sunny Says statements like "take your sunglasses off."

At Sci-Port, the children were given a craft exercise, in which they made their own sun hat. With the help of an adult, each child cut off the rim of a paper plate and used a hot glue gun to attach the rim to a paper bowl to make the hat. Then, they could decorate their hat using markers, glitter, and other craft items. Colorful yarn was also available to attach to the hat rim, so that the hat could be secured to the child's head. For an example, see figure 5.3.

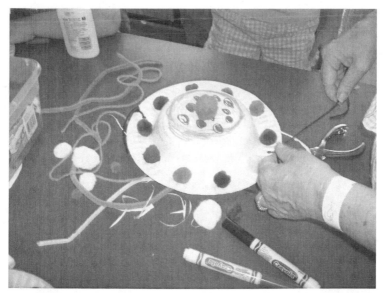

Figure 5.3.   With the help of adults, children create their own sun hats (© 2010, Donna F. Timm)

Sleep Habits

A story hour about healthy sleep habits was conducted for the first time in December 2014 to correspond with Christmas, since Santa will not visit your house until everyone is asleep. Library faculty began the story time by reading the classic poem "'Twas the Night before Christmas" to make the connection between healthy sleep habits and Santa's annual visit. Then, they read other sleep-related stories, which are listed in the appendix. For the activity, they once again adapted the Simon Says game to create Santa Says. In this activity, the children followed Santa's advice for getting a good night's rest and ignored the bad habits that disrupt sleep patterns, such as playing video games before bedtime.

The librarians also created a coloring sheet using Microsoft ClipArt depicting a sleeping cat with the words "Quiet Please. It is Time to Sleep." Each child was given a coloring sheet, construction paper, and yarn to make their own "Do Not Disturb" sign to hang on their bedroom door while they are sleeping.

Dental Health

For the first time in 2015, librarians taught a lesson about proper dental hygiene. They purchased an adorable dinosaur puppet with large protruding teeth that could easily be used to demonstrate proper brushing and flossing. They affectionately named the puppet "Toothy the T-Rex." Even though the librarians had no training as ventriloquists, they still created a voice for the puppet. Luckily, the children were so mesmerized by "Toothy" that they did not seem to notice the librarian's mouth moving.

Rather than purchasing an expensive puppet stage, the library faculty used their portable healthelinks display (see figure 5.4). The librarian and "Toothy" sat facing the front of the display, while the back of the display faced the children. This arrangement provided the coverage needed to hide the puppet master's arm. During her conversation with "Toothy," the librarian taught him how to brush his teeth and floss using a one-handed floss pick, since the librarian only had one available arm. The children loved "Toothy" and even wanted to pet him after the story hour ended.

PROMOTION AND PUBLICITY

As mentioned previously, the librarians used the healthelinks For Kids web portal to advertise the story times and follow-up activities as well as to provide contact information for the LSU Health Shreveport librarians and the children's librarians. In addition, the librarians promoted the story times through their partner institutions: the Shreve Memorial Library system and

Figure 5.4.   Portable healthelinks display (© 2013, Deidra Woodson)

Sci-Port. Bookmarks advertising the web portal were created, and the library's consumer health website, healthelinks, was promoted through exhibits at some of the story times and summer reading program venues.

The story times and other events were publicized on the LSU Health Shreveport Facebook page and on the library's website. Media coverage was provided by three local television stations and the newspaper; the cover story of an electronic newsletter, the *LSU System Media Sweep*; and a rotating banner on the healthelinks web portal.

RESULTS AND REWARDS

The LSU Health Shreveport librarians are delighted that their program has been so successful and has reached so many children in the local community. To date, the librarians have conducted forty-five children's health events at seven different locations and have taught nearly four thousand children. The lowest attendance at a story time was a mere six children, but the greatest attendance was two hundred-thirty children. The latter group was divided into two smaller groups due to the overwhelming number. The children's librarian at the Shreve Memorial Library Wallette Branch entertained one group of children, while the LSU Health Shreveport librarians taught the other group.

The children were engaged and enthusiastically participated in the activities. Although no formal evaluation was conducted, the children were asked questions throughout the programs to test their retention of the material covered. Based on their correct responses to these questions, the children were obviously learning while having fun. Seeing the children smiling and learning was very rewarding for the librarians. In addition, the librarians were able to reach children with various disabilities at Sci-Port. Observing these special needs children participating in the activities was also a very gratifying experience.

Overall, the children were entertained while learning about nutrition, exercise, and other healthy habits. Their teachers and the public librarians were presented with activities and ideas that could be incorporated into future programs. As long as the children, their teachers, and the public librarians continue to respond positively and welcome the events, the medical librarians hope to continue this outreach program.

LESSONS LEARNED

The health sciences librarians have continued to maintain and update this project since it began in 2009, so it has obviously been rewarding in many ways; however, no project is without its challenges, and this one is no exception. A few of the challenges encountered are listed below.

- Be choosy. Collaborating with the right partners is essential for any consumer health initiative. For this project, the first challenge encountered was to select the appropriate library branches that serve the target population and have well-developed children's programs. Connecting with branch managers who can provide information on the populations served as well as programs already taking place can assist in the decision-making process. By participating in or enhancing existing programs, librarians will have a built-in audience for the new programming to be offered.
- Be flexible. Ideally, those planning the programs should have an estimate of the number of expected attendees. However, attendance can

vary, even with well-established programs. For example, the librarians encountered groups as small as six children and as large as two hundred-thirty, and this presented a challenge in terms of selecting stories to accommodate the wide range of group sizes. Nevertheless, this issue can be dealt with by having more than one librarian prepared to assist with the program on those days when the groups might be larger than expected.

- Be prepared. When conducting programs for the public, unexpected situations can occur. Since young children are unpredictable, the librarians had to be prepared to handle any situation. Sometimes the children were very well behaved but at other times, their attention span was short. Luckily, their preschool teachers were in attendance and could discipline them as needed. Of course, librarians can also deal with disciplinary issues by requiring that the students settle down before continuing the story or activity, a technique that usually works well.
- Be resourceful. When preparing for an educational event, search for existing materials that can be used or adapted as needed. For the story times, the librarians strove to select books that were appropriate to the health-related theme, easy to read aloud, written for young children, and also available in the public library system with which they collaborated. Some stories selected were appropriate, but included some content that was either too complicated for young children or conveyed information interfering with the overall health lesson. When reading these stories, the librarians simply skipped the inappropriate parts. Furthermore, on some topics such as sun safety, there were few appropriate story books available. On that topic, one librarian wrote a story and another illustrated it, which was a creative solution to the problem.
- Be creative. When designing programs, the activities should be appropriate for any size group and for the space available. Librarians planned follow-up activities to reinforce concepts presented in the stories, but it became a challenge to plan activities that could be implemented in groups of varying sizes and to produce an adequate number of handouts to support these activities. Librarians addressed these issues by designing some activities that could be done within the space available and other activities that could be completed later when the preschoolers returned to their own institutions. Their teachers were pleased to have additional activities for the children, and the preschoolers had a second opportunity to learn about the concepts presented during story time.

Despite the fact that these challenges existed, they were minor roadblocks when compared to the overall rewards of the project.

CONCLUSION

When the library faculty began this project six years ago, there were no plans to continue it indefinitely; however, that is what has happened. The project has been so well received by the partners with whom the librarians have collaborated that the story times continue to be offered today. Not only have the library faculty enjoyed long-term success with this project, but also the children have benefited from its continued success, as evidenced by their joyful responses to the follow-up activities and the question-and-answer sessions that follow each health-related story presented.

This long-term project has given the library faculty many opportunities to interact with children who were engaged in the health-related stories and activities. Furthermore, the extensive media coverage provided visibility to the library's outreach efforts in the local community.

The LSU Health Shreveport librarians plan to continue to work on this project with their existing partners, establish additional partnerships, explore new themes, acquire new stories to update their children's health book collection, and develop more follow-up activities to reinforce the lessons from the stories.

APPENDIX: RECOMMENDED STORIES

General Wellness

Oh, the Things You Can Do That Are Good for You! by Tish Rabe; illustrated by Aristides Ruiz. New York: Random House, 2001.

The Cat in the Hat takes the reader on an adventure to an entertaining health spa. The fun characters demonstrate how to stay healthy. This book covers nutrition, exercise, germs, sleep habits, dental hygiene, body image, and more. The children are easily entertained by the Seuss-style rhyming and entertaining characters. However, the book contains the 1993 food pyramid established by the United States Department of Agriculture (USDA). Despite this dated information, the story is still highly recommended.

Nutrition

Good Food by DeMar Reggier; illustrated by David Austin Clar. New York: Children's Press, 2005.

A young boy helps his father shop for healthy food at the grocery store. When they get home, they prepare a nutritious meal for the whole family. This book is written for very young readers, as the text is minimal. Although the story is simple, it provides the perfect transition to the Grocery Bag game.

Little Pea by Amy Krouse Rosenthal; illustrated by Jen Corace. San Francisco: Chronicle Books, 2005.

In this story, Little Pea does not want to eat his dinner, but his parents insist that he eat his meal so that he will grow up to be a strong pea. His unappetizing meal is candy, and his reward for eating his dinner is his favorite dessert, spinach. This story offers an entertaining twist to teach young children about nutrition.

Oliver's Vegetables by Vivian French; illustrated by Alison Bartlett. London: Hodder Children's Books, 1995.

Oliver only eats potato chips. His grandparents grow their vegetable garden, so when he stays with them for a week, he agrees to a compromise. If he can find the vegetable from which chips are made, then he can have chips. Otherwise, he must eat the vegetable he chooses. Throughout the week, he chooses a variety of vegetables, including carrots, beets, and spinach. Oliver learns that he likes other foods besides only potato chips. This cleverly written story was read as part of the garden-themed story hour that was developed for the "Dig into Reading" Collaborative Summer Library Program.

The Picky Little Witch by Elizabeth Brokamp; illustrated by Marsha Riti. Gretna, LA: Pelican Publishing, 2011.

Mama Witch tries to get her daughter to eat some Halloween soup before going out to trick-or-treat, but Picky Little Witch finds many reasons to refuse. By the end, Picky Little Witch realizes that the soup is better than she imagined. This book is ideal for creating a nutrition program conducted at Halloween, which is a time when many children eat too much candy. Unfortunately, in the second half of this story, Picky Little Witch convinces her mother to try a piece of candy after trick-or-treating. Since describing the wonderful flavor of sugar is counterproductive to the overall lesson, the librarians did not read this part of the story.

The Very Hungry Caterpillar by Eric Carle. New York: Philomel Books, 1987.

This story follows the life and eating habits of a caterpillar. Typically, the caterpillar eats fruits and leaves, but one day he eats too much junk food and gets a stomachache. This classic book not only teaches counting, but also provides a warning against overeating.

Why Can't I Have Cake for Dinner? adapted by Jodi Huelin from Jim Henson's *Sid the Science Kid*. New York: Collins, 2010.

It is Sid's birthday, and he wants cake for breakfast, lunch, and dinner. At school, his teacher explains why eating cake and other sugary foods all of the time is not healthy, and she teaches them about eating nutritious foods from each food group. When he gets home from school, Sid decides to have a healthy meal for dinner and save the cake for dessert. Children are immediately interested in this story because they recognize the characters from the familiar animated series.

Exercise

From Head to Toe by Eric Carle. New York: HarperCollins, 1997.

This is another classic story by Eric Carle that encourages the reader to imitate animal movements. Children have fun moving along with the animals, while learning anatomy and getting exercise.

Get Up and Go! by Nancy L. Carlson. New York: Puffin Books, 2006.

This story includes vibrant, fun-filled illustrations and an encouraging text that explains the many great reasons to exercise, from making new friends to going to new places to keeping your body healthy.

I.Q. Gets Fit by Mary Ann Fraser. New York: Walker & Company, 2007.

Even though I.Q. is the class pet mouse, he still wants to participate when the other students enroll in a school-wide fitness test. I.Q. learns about exercising and eating healthy foods. He works hard so that he can pass the test and win a ribbon. Even though he has difficulty keeping up with the rest of the children, he still succeeds, proving that anyone can become healthy. One disadvantage of the book is that it includes the 2005 food pyramid, which preceded the current MyPlate guidelines set forth by the USDA.

Stretch by Doreen Cronin; illustrated by Scott Menchin. New York: Atheneum Books, 2009.

A cute dog instructs the reader to perform a number of different and interesting stretches. This book helps preschoolers become more limber and is perfect to read as part of an exercise-themed story hour, as it allows the children to stretch prior to the main physical activity.

Wallie Exercises by Steve Ettinger; illustrated by Pete Proctor. New York: Active Spud Press, 2011.

Wallie is a great dog, but he has gotten too lazy and overweight. His owner takes him to the park to get fit. They meet an elephant, who teaches Wallie that exercising does not have to be difficult, especially if you discover activities that you actually enjoy.

Hand Hygiene

Germs Are Not for Sharing by Elizabeth Verdick; illustrated by Marieka Heinlen. Minneapolis: Free Spirit Publishing, 2006.

In this book, the writer explains that sharing germs can spread illness and describes various ways that germs are transferred from one person to another, such as touching doorknobs, toys, and pets. The writer also explains how to prevent the spread of germs. This book provides simple explanations and illustrations that are easy to understand.

Germs! Germs! Germs! by Bobbi Katz; illustrated by Steve Björkman. New York: Scholastic, 1996.

In this rhyming story, germs do the talking. They describe where they live and how they travel. They also explain that they do not like soap and water. This is a unique story that offers a different method for teaching proper hygiene.

A Germ's Journey by Thom Rooke; illustrated by Tony Trimmer. North Mankato, MN: Picture Windows Book, 2011.

The germs in this story begin their journey by parachuting out of a sick student's nose during an uncovered sneeze. The germs land on other students and ordinary objects. Some students wash their hands, but others do not. Eventually, they travel from one person to another and beyond, spreading illness wherever they go. This book effectively explains how disease is transmitted without being overly didactic.

Wash Your Hands! by Margaret McNamara; illustrated by Mike Gordon. New York: Simon Spotlight, 2010.

This easy-to-read story takes place in a classroom setting, where every student has a cold. The teacher uses this opportunity to demonstrate proper hand-washing techniques. This is another effective book that includes a hand-washing song.

Heart Health

Hear Your Heart by Paul Showers; illustrated by Holly Keller. New York: HarperCollins, 2001.

This book includes a detailed description of the heart and its functions, and it effectively explains the importance of the heart. At times, though, the explanations seem overly complicated for preschoolers. Therefore, these sections are omitted during readings. However, this book describes how a cardboard tube can be used as a stethoscope, which provides an effective transition to the stethoscope craft activity.

Thump-Thump: Learning about Your Heart by Pamela Hill Nettleton; illustrated by Becky Shipe. Minneapolis: Picture Window Books, 2004.

This book explains the functions of the heart in plain language, but it also includes details that may be too complex for preschoolers. The more complicated sections are not read during the story hours. At the end of this book, the author briefly describes how to keep your heart healthy, so that it will continue to work properly.

Sleep Habits

My Dad Is Big and Strong, But . . . : A Bedtime Story by Coralie Saudo; illustrated by Kris Di Giacomo. New York: Enchanted Lion Books, 2012.

In this story, a little boy has trouble putting his dad to bed, as his dad refuses to go to sleep. Even though the boy's father is big and strong, he is afraid of the dark. The little boy turns on a nightlight, and his father finally goes to sleep. By changing the perspective from parent to child, this story cleverly informs children to communicate with their parents at bedtime, rather than simply resisting them.

Nighty-Night, Cooper by Laura Numeroff; illustrated by Lynn Munsinger. Boston: Houghton Mifflin Books for Children, 2013.

Cooper is a young kangaroo who cannot go to sleep. His mother tries singing lullabies to help him sleep, but he keeps requesting more songs. Finally, his mother tells him to sing his own lullaby, and then, he falls asleep. This adorable story provides another option to assist children with going to bed. However, the reader should be willing to sing the songs during the story time.

Dental Health

Brush Your Teeth Please by Leslie McGuire; illustrated by Jean Pidgeon. White Plains, NY: Reader's Digest Children's Books, 2013.

This is an interactive pop-up book, in which various animals are shown cleaning their teeth. On each page, the animal is brushing a different part of the mouth, and the reader can move the toothbrush to see it in action. The book also includes a section about flossing, in which the reader can use the attached strings to floss the animal's teeth. Children are easily entertained by this pop-up book, while learning how to care for their teeth.

Elmo Visits the Dentist by P. J. Shaw; illustrated by Tom Brannon. Franklin, TN: Dalmatian Press, 2012.

The Big Bad Wolf has a tooth ache, so Elmo helps Big Bad by taking him to see the dentist. Big Bad learns how to take care of his teeth by eating healthy foods and cleaning his teeth. Since the children love the familiar Sesame Street characters, they are very interested in this story.

The Teeth That Looked for a New Mouth: A Story of a Boy Who Didn't Like to Brush His Teeth by Jill Jones; illustrated by Emily Zieroth. Lexington, KY: [Self Published using CreateSpace], 2014.

Luke does not like to brush his teeth, so his teeth get very dirty. One night, he dreams that his teeth are so tired of being dirty that they leave to look for a new, clean mouth. By the end of his dream, his teeth found an elderly man with only a few teeth and would love to have a full set of teeth again. When Luke awakens from his nightmare, he rushes to the bathroom to clean his teeth. This story entertains and educates children about proper dental health by providing the perspective of the teeth.

REFERENCES

Alvin and the Chipmunks. 1999. "The Alvin Twist." *Greatest Hits: Still Squeaky After All These Years*. Capitol Records. MP3 file downloaded from Amazon.

Amini, Maryam, Abolghassem Djazayery, Reza Majdzadeh, Mohammad-Hossein Taghdisi, and Shima Jazayeri. 2015. "Effect of School-Based Interventions to Control Childhood Obesity: A Review of Reviews." *International Journal of Preventive Medicine* 6, no. 1 (August): 68–83.

Brown, Callie L., Elizabeth E. Halvorson, Gail M. Cohen, Suzanne Lazorick, and Joseph A. Skelton. 2015. "Addressing Childhood Obesity: Opportunities for Prevention." *Pediatric Clinics of North America* 62, no. 5 (October): 1241–61.

Daniels, Stephen R. 2006. "The Consequences of Childhood Overweight and Obesity." *Future Child* 16, no. 1 (Spring): 47–67.

EPA (Environmental Protection Agency). 2014. "SunWise: Sample Classroom Activity for Grades K–2." Environmental Protection Agency. Last updated November 28. http://www2.epa.gov/sunwise/sunwise-sample-classroom-activity-grades-k-2.

Guinan, Maryellen, Maryanne McGuckin, and Yusef Ali. 2002. "The Effect of a Comprehensive Handwashing Program on Absenteeism in Elementary Schools." *American Journal of Infection Control* 30, no. 4 (June): 217–20.

Gurnani, Muskaan, Catherine Birken, and Jill Hamilton. 2015. "Childhood Obesity: Causes, Consequences, and Management." *Pediatric Clinics of North America* 62, no. 4 (August): 821–40.

Han, Joan C., Debbie A. Lawlor, and Sue Y. S. Kimm. 2010. "Childhood Obesity." *Lancet* 375, no. 9727 (May): 1737–48.

Hughes, Adrienne R., Andrea Sherriff, Andrew R. Ness, and John J. Reilly. 2014. "Timing of Adiposity Rebound and Adiposity in Adolescence." *Pediatrics* 134, no. 5 (November): 1354–61.

Kumanyika, Shiriki, and Sonya Grier. 2006. "Targeting Interventions for Ethnic Minority and Low-Income Populations." *Future Child* 16, no. 1 (Spring): 187–207.

LSU Health Shreveport Health Sciences Library. 2015. "healthelinks Selection Criteria." healthelinks. http://www.healthelinks.org/criteria.html.

Mahar, Matthew T., Rhonda K. Kenny, A. Tamlyn Shields, Donna P. Scales, and Gretchen Collins. 2015. "Energizers: Classroom-Based Physical Activities." East Carolina University. Accessed September 5, 2015. https://www.ecu.edu/cs-hhp/exss/upload/Energizers_for_Grades_K_2.pdf.

Ng, Marie, Tom Fleming, Margaret Robinson, et al. 2014. "Global, Regional, and National Prevalence of Overweight and Obesity in Children and Adults during 1980–2013: A Systematic Analysis for the Global Burden of Disease Study 2013." *Lancet* 384, no. 9945 (August-September): 766–81.

Ogden, Cynthia L., Margaret D. Carroll, Brian K. Kit, and Katherine M. Flegal. 2014. "Prevalence of Childhood and Adult Obesity in the United States, 2011–2012." *JAMA: Journal of the American Medical Association* 311, no. 8 (February): 806–14.

Safron, Magdalena, Aleksandra Cislak, Tania Gaspar, and Aleksandra Luszczynska. 2011. "Effects of School-Based Interventions Targeting Obesity-Related Behaviors and Body Weight Change: A Systematic Umbrella Review." *Behavioral Medicine* 37, no. 1 (January): 15–25.

Serdula, M. K., D. Ivery, R. J. Coates, D. S. Freedman, D. F. Williamson, and T. Byers. 1993. "Do Obese Children Become Obese Adults? A Review of the Literature." *Preventive Medicine* 22, no. 2 (March): 167–77.

Skinner, Asheley Cockrell, and Joseph A. Skelton. 2014. "Prevalence and Trends in Obesity and Severe Obesity among Children in the United States, 1999–2012." *JAMA Pediatrics* 168, no. 6 (June): 561–66.

Woodson, Deidra, Dee Jones, and Donna F. Timm. 2012. "Playing Online Interactive Games for Health Education: Evaluating Their Effectiveness." *Journal of Hospital Librarianship* 12, no. 4 (October–December): 351–62.

6

Collaborative Outreach between a Hospital Library and a Public Library

MARGOT MALACHOWSKI, *Baystate Health*;
ANNE GANCARZ, *Chicopee Public Library*;
ELLEN BRASSIL, *Baystate Health*

Reliable information in support of self-empowerment is a critical part of the consumer movement in general and readily applies to consumer health information (CHI). Consumer rights and responsibilities are reflected in informed consent laws, patients' rights, and other concepts where patients and their families take part in decision making to achieve greater autonomy. Yet, accessing reliable CHI is challenging in today's flood of information. This situation is compounded by the vulnerability of persons and families facing serious illness or major medical procedures. For those who lack mobility or transportation, or have difficulties navigating print or electronic resources, the challenges are even greater. Hospital librarians are highly skilled in helping community members find reliable CHI. Impressive examples of health literacy outreach are well covered in the literature, measured in terms of patient satisfaction, health status, improved communication, or communication with providers (Bandy, 2015; Berkman et al., 2011; McKnight, 2014; Smith and Duman, 2009).

Despite these successes, hospital libraries face distinct obstacles in reaching vulnerable community members. Hospital libraries lack the advantages found at public libraries, such as convenient location, parking, and operating hours. In fact, public libraries are providing their communities with CHI and are oftentimes the first line of service in the community member's quest to learn more about a given health topic (Huber and Gillaspy, 2011). Collaboration between hospital and public libraries strengthens the efforts of both institutions to support consumer self-empowerment. By developing a playbook, a set of strategies used for outlining a campaign (Dictionary.com, 2015), the libraries plan to enhance community outreach by basing new efforts upon existing institutional data. This chapter will describe consumer health information programs at both Baystate Health and at a nearby public library, and the team building between both libraries to bring data-driven outreach to the community.

CONSUMER HEALTH LIBRARY AT BAYSTATE HEALTH

Baystate Health (BH) is a not-for-profit, integrated health system operating in Hampden, Hampshire, and Franklin counties in western Massachusetts. BH's facilities include Baystate Medical Center (BMC), the region's only Level I Trauma center, and Baystate Children's Hospital, as well as four community hospitals, over eighty medical practices, and home health care. All BH facilities are served by the Health Sciences Library (HSL) at the BMC campus. HSL is a Resource Library for the National Network of Libraries in Medicine (NN/LM). The mission of the NN/LM is to advance the progress of medicine and improve public health by providing all health care providers in the United States with equal access to biomedical information, and improving the public's access to CHI to enable them to make informed decisions (NN/LM, 2015). This mission is consistent with HSL's own mission.

HEALTH SCIENCES LIBRARY MISSION

"The Health Sciences Library, comprised of the Baystate Medical Center Library and the Consumer Health Library at 3300 Main Street, provides information support for all Baystate Health providers, faculty, students, and staff. HSL services are designed to anticipate and be responsive to the individual's information needs for teaching, learning, research and the highest quality healthcare. Additionally, the HSL serves the health sciences information needs of Baystate Health overall, and provides appropriate access to selected resources and services for the general healthcare community and the public." (Baystate Health Sciences Library, 2010)

HSL operates a small satellite Consumer Health Library (CHL) in the Tolosky Center, a medical practices building at 3300 Main Street in Springfield. CHL is a free service for patients, their families, and the community at large. Created in 1998, the intention of CHL is to provide a physical location for accessing CHI. The operating hours are Monday–Friday 12 noon–5 PM. CHL is staffed by the Community Outreach Librarian.

Measuring at 534 square feet, CHL has a reading room atmosphere with a table and chairs, and soft chairs in front of a fireplace. Visitors have access to anatomy textbooks, medical dictionaries, diagnosis and treatment guidebooks, health care provider directories, medical translation dictionaries, drug handbooks, integrative medicine guidebooks, and books on selected health concerns (e.g., diabetes, multiple sclerosis, and thyroid disorders). The collection includes health letters from the Mayo Clinic, Johns Hopkins, Harvard Medical, University of California at Berkeley, *Consumer Reports*, and the Center for Science in the Public Interest. Over twenty anatomy models and flipcharts are available. CHL offers free pamphlets on over thirty topics related to general health.

There are two computers available to access subscription databases licensed by HSL. Computer print-outs and photocopies are free of charge. Many visitors take advantage of the Wi-Fi connection when using personal laptops and tablets. The Community Outreach Librarian does not offer medical advice or patient education, but rather guidance in the selection of CHI materials. By offering computer access and guidance on selecting resources, CHL specifically focuses on the Healthy People 2020 Health Communication/Health Information Technology Objectives HC/HIT-6: "Increase individuals' access to the Internet," and HC/HIT-9: "Increase the proportion of online health information seekers who report easily accessing health information" (Healthy People 2020, 2015).

The most frequently requested health topics by walk-ins are anatomy images, condition-specific diets, and disease management information on heart disease, dementia, cancer, and allergies. For each question, several documents are selected and printed out by the librarian. CHL handles requests by phone and e-mail as well. The librarian fulfills phone/e-mail requests by performing more detailed searches, and mailing or e-mailing relevant documents. These detailed searches are typically for chronic conditions, such as heart failure, migraines, and diabetes.

In addition to providing library access for twenty-five hours per week, the Community Outreach Librarian attends health fairs, teaches health information classes, and participates in community health coalition meetings. Performing outreach requires diligence in searching for potential venues and partnerships. A significant part of the librarian's job is maintaining current awareness of local events, nurturing existing relationships with community partners, and initiating contact with potential community partners. In recent years, HSL partnered with the Springfield Department of Elder Affairs, The Literacy Project, Springfield Technical Community College, and several public libraries.

BAYSTATE HEALTH TEAMS UP WITH CHICOPEE PUBLIC LIBRARY

The first collaboration between HSL and Chicopee Public Library (CPL) occurred in 2013. After a successful program with Springfield City Libraries

in 2010, HSL hoped to replicate the collaboration with other public librar-
ies. The program, *Community Engagement: Collaboration between Baystate
Health Sciences Library and Springfield City Library to Teach MedlinePlus*,
comprised a series of six classes on finding reliable health information on
the Internet taught by a medical librarian in a public library computer lab.
Each class focused on a health concern, such as Heart Health, Diabetes, and
Healthy Weight. This program received partial funding from the National
Network of Libraries of Medicine—New England Region. To seek new partners, librarians at HSL searched online for Hampden County public libraries with active adult programming. After gaining a perspective on potential
partners, HSL posted an offer for multi-library collaboration on the statewide
listserv (allregions@mblc.state.ma.us). Librarians at the Chicopee Public
Library, located less than five miles from HSL, responded.

Chicopee Public Library (CPL) opened a beautiful new 31,600-square-
foot building in 2004. The upper level houses the Children's Room, circulation services, the fiction collection, audiovisual materials, public access
computers, new materials, and the young adult collection. Reference services, the reference collection, nonfiction collection, public access computers, and periodicals are on the lower level. Also located on the lower level
are the computer lab, several meeting rooms, and the local history collection. After the opening of the new building, CPL experienced steady growth
in the circulation of materials and borrower registration. The new meeting
rooms and an outdoor amphitheater contributed to an explosion of adult and
children's programming (Chicopee Public Library, 2015). CPL has one
branch library, located within the Fairhaven Housing complex, and
launched bookmobile services in the summer of 2015.

In addition to the branch library and the bookmobile, CPL employs a Community Services Librarian to take library resources and services to locations

---

CHICOPEE PUBLIC LIBRARY MISSION

"The Chicopee Public Library embraces the spirit of the Chicopee community by
providing materials and services to contribute to and enhance personal enrich-
ment, enjoyment, and educational endeavors. The library supports lifelong learning and information literacy by providing computer access, print and online
information resources, an active website and ongoing review of new technologies.
Community centered activities include extensive adult and children's programming, reference assistance, computer classes, meeting room facilities, outreach
services, and collaborations with city departments, library consortiums, and community agencies." (Chicopee Public Library, 2011)

such as the Chicopee Council of Aging and Chicopee Public Schools. CPL works strategically to meet the needs of the city, basing initial decisions on an informal community assessment performed in 2008. The purpose of the assessment was to identify unmet needs for library services. An informal assessment includes suggestions from the community, observations in the community, and anecdotal information that would suggest a need for services (Rubin, 2001). In this instance, CPL made phone calls to every public library in the cities and towns abutting Chicopee. The librarians discussed types of services, including outreach, currently offered by each library. Many valuable conversations took place. Based upon the information gathered, CPL created a framework for public service that focuses on providing library services to the traditionally underserved. For example, proposed outreach initiatives included enhancing library services for the blind community, ex-offenders, homebound patrons, and adult learners. Although the identified populations are considerably different from each other, the role of the librarian remains the same—to provide library services in a setting that is responsive to their needs and in a respectful manner. This includes provision of CHI.

Like many public libraries, CPL offers a variety of health-related library collections, programming, and services. CPL has a deep investment in providing current, accurate health-related information. As such, the library ensures the availability of current print and electronic resources and invites health care professionals to offer programs. The senior reference librarian selects titles for the nonfiction and reference collection. Results from a survey conducted in 2008 determined that top health interests are diet/nutrition, fitness/exercise, alternative health remedies, stress management, smoking cessation, and disease-specific information. The most popular reference questions include heart disease, diabetes, cancer, mental illness, as well as nutrition and health-promoting behavior. Patrons continually ask for assistance in finding disease-specific and healthy living resources, often requesting items that are culturally popular but not evidence-based science. CPL purchases books that are reputable and recommended, and allows some leeway for patron requests for items seen on television or read about in a weekly magazine. Depending upon the volume of requests on a particular topic, CPL may invite a guest speaker to the library. For example, a surge in requests for alternative treatment for ADHD resulted in a well-attended talk given by a naturopathic doctor.

Several databases are frequently recommended to patrons seeking current and succinct information. Reference librarians will search and print materials to fill the patron's request. These databases, available through the library website (http://www.chicopeepubliclibrary.org), are listed in the textbox.

DATABASES AVAILABLE FROM CHICOPEE PUBLIC LIBRARY

- Gale Health & Wellness Resource Center (http://www.gale.com)
- Gale Health Reference Center (http://www.gale.com)
- Gale Physical Therapy & Sports Medicine Collection (http://www.gale.com)
- Gale Nursing Resource Center (http://www.gale.com)
- National Library of Medicine MedlinePlus (http://www.medlineplus.gov)
- Rosen Teen Health & Wellness (http://www.teenhealthandwellness.com)

The chief aim of the initial collaboration between HSL and CPL was to bring the expertise of the medical librarian into the public library setting. This would allow CPL to expand health-related programming with no cost to the municipality. HSL would gain a new venue for community outreach, with a goal of supporting BH's community benefit mission to reduce health disparities, promote community wellness, and improve access to care for vulnerable populations (Verité Heathcare Consultants, 2013). As Chicopee represents nearly 12 percent of Hampden County's population, and ranks second in the county for BMC patient discharges, conducting outreach at CHL proved to be a great match (Verité Heathcare Consultants, 2013). Ultimately, the collaboration led to a "meeting of the minds" between the medical librarian and the public librarian, fostering a mutual commitment to addressing local CHI needs through multi-library collaboration. Mutual objectives were:

- Support the CHI needs of community members as they grapple with medical decisions.
- Provide support in an environment most comfortable for the community members.
- Utilize the strengths of each library type to enhance CHI delivery.

PLAYBOOK FOR DATA-DRIVEN OUTREACH

HSL offered classes in the CPL computer lab in March 2014, July 2014, and February 2015. Each time, enrollment was low, with an average of two participants. The librarians decided to go back to the drawing board to design a new strategy for promoting CHI. Using techniques recommended by independent library consultant Rhea Joyce Rubin (Rubin, 2001) and the *Planning and Evaluating Health Information Outreach Projects* booklets freely available from the Outreach Evaluation Resource Center of the NN/LM (Olney and Barnes, 2013), the librarians embarked on the planning process to design a collaborative outreach program featuring the CPL's new bookmobile (see figure 6.1). This was the start of the data-driven playbook for community outreach.

Figure 6.1. Chicopee Public Library Bookmobile (Credit: Chicopee Public Library. Used with permission)

The CPL Bookmobile had a very successful inaugural year, with circulation statistics rivaling the branch library. The Bookmobile began its route in June 2015 with a biweekly schedule of two ninety-minute stops per day, visiting neighborhoods throughout Chicopee. The route included weekly visits to the local farmer's market and the Chicopee Council on Aging, as well as rotational visits to the city parks, local Boys & Girls Club, and federally assisted housing complexes. The Bookmobile made special appearances at city-sponsored outdoor movie nights and National Night Out, America's Night Out against Crime. Within eight weeks, the Bookmobile engaged 1,747 community members with access to Wi-Fi hot spots, four iPads, a large touch screen computer, and a full-service circulation desk. The collection of two thousand items included bestselling novels, children's chapter books and picture books, a teen book and graphic novel collection, DVDs, audio books, nonfiction books, large-print books, magazines, paperback novels, and a small collection of adult readers (books specifically designed for adults who are learning to read and/or learning English).

The aim of the data-driven playbook is to plan how to combine the best practices of the CPL Bookmobile and the outreach strategies of HSL to enhance CHI outreach. The HSL finds that getting out of the library to participate in community health fairs substantially increases community awareness of and access to CHI services. HSL recorded a sharp increase in requests for CHI from 2011 to 2014. By boosting yearly participation from two to six health fairs, HSL received 65 percent more CHI requests and quadrupled the repeat customer requests. These requests included phone and e-mail queries, as well as Information Rx forms filled out by community members at the health fairs. The use of Information Rx forms revolutionized community participation at the HSL health fair table. While community members browse the available pamphlets, the librarian offers to research any health topic and send results in the mail. Interested community members will self-address a large envelope while the librarian jots down the topic on the Information Rx pad. The Rx form is slipped into the envelope, facilitating the fulfilling of the request upon return to the library. This interaction demonstrates the services of the library beyond the provision of materials. The data-driven playbook is based upon the idea of creating similar interactions on the CPL Bookmobile.

Data on Health Care Priorities for Hampden County

The first step in any data-driven plan is to gather information (Rubin, 2001). The librarians have easy access to circulation statistics, popular topics, reference statistics, and CPL's informal community assessment and formal long-range plan. To home in on potential CHI needs, the next step was to consult the 2013 Community Health Needs Assessment (CHNA) for Hampden County. The CHNA revealed that the community has a growing population of Asians and Latinos. Projections for 2017 indicate that the Asian population will grow almost 15 percent from 2012 to 2017, and Latinos will account for 24.5 percent of the population. Language and cultural barriers complicate interactions with health care providers. Hampden County has high rates of disability, with 16.8 percent reporting hearing difficulty, vision difficulty, cognitive disability, ambulatory difficulty, self-care difficulty, and/ or independent living difficulty. This compares with 11.3 percent for Massachusetts and 12.1 percent for the United States. Hampden County is more reliant on government support programs, such as the Supplemental Nutrition Assistance Program (SNAP) and Temporary Assistance for Needy Families (TANF) than the average for Massachusetts communities. Limited access to mental health services disproportionately affects these low-income community members. High rates of teen pregnancy and smoking during pregnancy contribute to notable poor infant outcomes within the county. The incidence of obesity, diabetes, and cardiovascular disease is higher than state averages (Verité Healthcare Consultants, 2013). By focusing on the known prevalence of disease and barriers to health care access in Hampden County, the HSL and CPL librarians are better positioned to meet the CHI needs of local underserved populations (Tennant, 2014).

Data on Library Partners Delivering Consumer Health Information

HSL and CPL embarked upon a partnership with a shared desire to heighten the visibility of CHI services. At the ground level, each library became better acquainted with currently existing services. Medical librarians may not be aware of the changing role of public libraries. Far from being yesterday's news, today's public libraries are thriving. Between the years 2002 and 2012, visits to U.S. public libraries grew by 10.1 percent. Library collections expanded, in particular video materials (86.9 percent), audio materials (94 percent), and electronic books (1,744 percent). Public access computers grew by 76.1 percent during that same time period (Swan et al., 2014). Public libraries are providing workspace for telecommuters. By offering access to 3D printers and other technology tools, some public libraries are exploring opportunities to be makerspaces (Garmer, 2014). Medical librarians will find dynamic partnerships among today's public librarians.

Public librarians may be unaware of the community outreach needs of the local medical librarian. The Patient Protection and Affordable Care Act requires not-for-profit hospitals to conduct a CHNA every three years. The CHNA uses quantitative and qualitative methods to collect and analyze data related to community health. The definition of health is broad and considers social determinants of health (e.g., safe housing, exposure to toxins, violent crime, and residential segregation) as well as public health indicators (e.g., rates of heart disease, asthma, low birth weight, and life expectancy). In order to maintain tax-exempt status, hospitals must adopt an implementation strategy for community benefits programs that explicitly and publicly meet community health needs identified in the CHNA (Verité Healthcare Consultants, 2013). Nationwide, medical libraries are contributing to community benefits programs by documenting the provision of CIII.

Public librarians are wise to investigate local community benefits reports, required by law to be available on the hospital's website. At the very least, public librarians will learn more about the goals of these anchor institutions. The medical library might welcome the opportunity to distribute CHI resources, provide instruction in finding reliable health information, or offer expert reference services to librarians and/or the public. The possibility exists for greater involvement, as Pima County (Arizona) Library (PCPL) discovered in 2012 (Johnson, Mathewson, and Prechtel, 2014). PCPL was given the lead to address the need for health education and literacy for Pima County.

Learning about Chicopee Public Library

HSL discovered that CPL has a computer lab equipped with assistive technology for the blind, active adult programming, and ongoing health screenings for seniors. The Community Services Librarian has established partnerships in Hampden County, most notably with the disabled community. CPL was awarded funding from the Massachusetts Board of Library Commissioners in 2010 to enhance services to people with disabilities. Based on community input, the library made the decision to focus on services to patrons who are blind and patrons who are deaf or hard of hearing. Purchases included JAWS screen reading software and a portable Infrared Listening System (ILS). As a result, the computer lab is actively and vigorously used by people who are blind as they take part in classes and recreation on the computer. The ILS is used during lectures, movies, and classes to enhance the library experience for the hard of hearing. Thus, HSL learned that CPL is making valuable inroads with an identified underserved population.

Learning about Baystate Health Sciences Library

Chicopee Public Library discovered that the Health Sciences Library at Baystate Health is a resource to public librarians in Hampden County. As previously mentioned, HSL teaches classes on finding CHI in public library settings. The community outreach librarian provides in-service training to librarians through the Massachusetts Library System (a state-supported collaborative providing services to all Massachusetts libraries), the National Network of Libraries of Medicine—New England Region, and as a guest lecturer for Simmons College School of Library and Information Science. HSL welcomes referrals from public librarians, as well as requests on behalf of a library patron. HSL is an integral part of the CHNA process at Baystate Health. The community outreach librarian serves on the Steering Committee, which prepares documents for presentation to the executive leadership of Baystate Health. CPL learned that HSL is committed to leveraging partnerships that, according to Margaret Bandy, create "the energy of collaboration," and help shape "a new vision that directs action" (2015: 5).

THE DATA-DRIVEN PLAYBOOK

After gathering information about the CHI services of HSL and CPL, and examining the Hampden County health care priorities, the librarians were ready to develop the data-driven playbook. Using a logic model (see table 6.1), the librarians outlined goals, inputs, activities, and outcomes. The playbook is entitled "Health Sciences Library Outreach on the Chicopee Public Library Bookmobile." The goals are to (1) increase community awareness of consumer health information services provided by libraries and (2) increase community access to reliable consumer health information services provided by libraries. Each partner materially invests in the program. As inputs, HSL contributes pamphlets, Information Rx pads, large envelopes, bookmarks, and business cards. CPL contributes the vehicle, Wi-Fi hot spot, iPads, and related

Table 6.1. Logic Model

Playbook: "Health Sciences Library Outreach on the Chicopee Public Library Bookmobile"

Goals:
1. Increase community awareness of consumer health information services provided by libraries.
2. Increase community access to reliable consumer health information services provided by libraries. Each partner materially invests in the program.

Inputs	Activities		Outcomes		
What we invest	What we do	Who we reach	Why we do it: Short-term	Why we do it: Intermediate	Why we do it: Long-term
HSL contributes pamphlets, Info Rx pads, large envelopes, bookmarks, business cards. HSL contributes librarian for scheduled visits, and to handle Info Rx requests. CPL contributes vehicle, Wi-Fi hot spot, librarian, CPL resources and services.	HSL selects and supplies pamphlets. HSL collects Info Rx/ envelopes. HSL handles requests/ mailings. HSL librarian makes scheduled visits to demo MedlinePlus on iPad. CPL librarian promotes and distributes pamphlets. CPL librarian handles requests as time permits.	Chicopee/Hampden County community members v siting: Boys and Girls Club City parks Councils on Aging Farmer's Market Federally funded housing complexes	Establish a baseline of CHI interactions through the number of iPad demonstrations and the number of Information Rx requests.	Measure community willingness to consider using libraries, including MedlinePlus, in meeting future CHI needs.	Measureable increase in community members reporting willingness to use library resources when facing medical decisions.

Assumptions:
HSL/CPL librarians will follow the procedures of the plan.
Community members will be interested in obtaining CHI from the Bookmobile.

External Factors:
(+) Participating in health fairs increases CHI requests.
(+) Bookmobile had a successful inaugural year.
(-) Unpredictability of community attendance at any outdoor event.
(-) Ebbs and flows of community interest in health topics.

circulating items. HSL and CPL invest their librarians' time and expertise. Each partner is responsible for identified activities. HSL selects pamphlets specifically targeted toward managing prevalent diseases, in English and in Spanish, and makes scheduled visits to demonstrate MedlinePlus on iPads and handle CHI requests and mailings. CPL promotes and distributes pamphlets, handling CHI requests as time permits. With these inputs and activities, HSL and CPL plan to bring CHI to neighborhoods throughout the city.

HSL and CPL identified the desired short-term, intermediate, and long-term outcomes. In the short-term, the desired outcome is to establish a baseline of CHI interactions through the number of iPad demonstrations and the number of Information Rx requests. The CHI pamphlets, and the Bookmobile itself, are primarily a gateway to introducing library services provided by HSL, CPL, and the National Library of Medicine through the website MedlinePlus. Intermediate outcomes are a measure of community willingness to consider using libraries, including MedlinePlus, in meeting future CHI needs. In the long-term, the desired outcome is a measureable increase in community members reporting willingness to use library resources when facing medical decisions. Studies have shown that clear and reliable CHI helps to restore patients' loss of control and is one of the most effective social supports for cancer patients in particular (Helgeson and Cohen, 1996). The librarians are teaming up to provide reliable CHI in hopes of supporting a positive patient experience and ultimately elevating the level of communication between patients and their health care providers in Hampden County.

The playbook rests on two major assumptions, and the success is influenced by several external factors. The first assumption is that HSL and CPL librarians will follow the procedures of the plan. The second assumption is that community members will be interested in obtaining CHI from the Bookmobile. Positive external factors include the experiences of both HSL and CPL with outreach. HSL discovered that participating in health fairs increases CHI requests. The Chicopee Bookmobile had a successful inaugural year. Negative external factors include the unpredictability of community attendance at any outdoor event, and the ebbs and flows of community interest in health topics. For 2015–2016, assumptions and external factors will be evaluated with a process assessment. Process assessment methods are geared toward monitoring implementation, describing quality of activities, and tracking barriers and challenges (Olney and Barnes, 2013). The data collected will be used for improvement in 2016–2017.

Sample process questions for the data-driven playbook are:

- How well did HSL and CPL follow the procedures of the plan?
- What factors increased or decreased the quality of CHI delivery?

- How many pamphlets were delivered?
- How many iPad demonstrations of MedlinePlus were performed?
- How many Information Rx requests were filled?
- What strategies worked well to attract community members?
- What barriers impacted the ability to attract community members?
- What situational factors (e.g., host location or weather) affected implementation?

LESSONS LEARNED IN PLANNING THE DATA-DRIVEN PLAYBOOK

Lessons learned in planning the data-driven playbook are threefold: build relationships; be resilient; and use available data.

1. Build Relationships. Learn about programs offered by local libraries of all types. Pick up the phone, or post an inquiry on a listserv to gather insights about the surrounding community. By teaming up, librarians take advantage of the connections already established with vulnerable populations. The librarians at the Health Sciences Library and the Chicopee Public Library discovered a shared commitment to community outreach.
2. Be Resilient. Do not be discouraged by low turnout numbers for community events. Experienced librarians know firsthand the power of showing up. Keep the lines of communication open and redirect efforts toward another outlet. HSL and CPL decided to offer CHI services outside of the library instead of in the computer lab.
3. Use Available Data. Ample data exist on community health interests. There was no need to reinvent the wheel. Check to see what data are being collected on requests for health information, popular health topics, and the local prevalence of disease. HSL and CPL tapped into recently performed formal and informal community assessments, including the CHNA for Hampden County.

The bottom line is that a team approach yields greater results in any effort to engage the community in learning about library CHI resources and services.

CONCLUSION

The Health Sciences Library at Baystate Health opened the Consumer Health Library nearly twenty years ago for CHI distribution to patients and families.

Chicopee Public Library has always provided consumer health information to residents of the city of Chicopee as part of standard public library practice. After experiencing low turnout at a collaborative event, the librarians reflected on individual successes and decided to take library resources and services into the community. They devised a playbook, basing strategies upon institutional data. HSL and CPL will use this playbook to combine the skills and materials of a hospital library and a public library to provide quality consumer health information. The proposed inputs and activities are to freely distribute CHI, in English and Spanish, to Chicopee's low-income neighborhoods. The playbook will be evaluated for the effectiveness of implementation, the quality of activities, and specifics of barriers and challenges. With a team approach, HSL and CPL will maintain a mutual commitment to support the self-empowerment of those living in Hampden County.

REFERENCES

Bandy, Margaret Moylan. 2015. "Pivoting: Leveraging Opportunities in a Turbulent Health Care Environment." *Journal of the Medical Library Association* 103, no. 1 (January): 3–13.

Baystate Health Sciences Library. 2010. "Mission Statement." Internal document.

Berkman, Nancy D., Stacey L. Sheridan, Katrina E. Donahue, David J. Halpern, and Karen Crotty. 2011. "Low Health Literacy and Health Outcomes: An Updated Systematic Review." *Annals of Internal Medicine* 97, no. 2: 97–107. doi:10.7326/0003-4819-155-2-201107190-00005.

Chicopee Public Library. 2011. *Long Range Plan 2011–2015*. Chicopee Public Library. http://www.chicopeepubliclibrary.org/libinfo.

Chicopee Public Library. 2015. "Chicopee Public Library Long Range Plan 2011–2015." Accessed September 10. http://chicopeepubliclibrary.org/sites/default/files/long_range_plan_package.pdf.

Dictionary.com. 2015. "Playbook." *Dictionary.com Unabridged*. Random House, Inc. Accessed September 6. http://dictionary.reference.com/browse/playbook.

Garmer, Amy K. 2014. *Rising to the Challenge, Re-Envisioning Public Libraries*. Washington, DC: The Aspen Institute.

Healthy People 2020. 2015. "2020 Topics and Objectives—Objectives A–Z." HealthyPeople.gov. Accessed September 2. http://www.healthypeople.gov/2020/topicsobjectives2020/default.

Helgeson, Vicki S., and Sheldon Cohen. 1996. "Social Support and Adjustment to Cancer: Reconciling Descriptive, Correlational, and Intervention Research." *Health Psychology* 2, no. 15: 135–48.

Huber, Jeffrey T., and Mary L. Gillaspy. 2011. "Knowledge/Power Transforming the Social Landscape: The Case of the Consumer Health Information Movement." *Library Quarterly: Information, Community, Policy* 81, no. 4: 405–30.

Johnson, Kenya, Amber Mathewson, and Karen Prechtel. 2014. "From Crisis to Collaboration: Pima County Public Library Partners with Health Department for Library Nurse Program." *Public Libraries* 53, no. 1: 32–35.

McKnight, Michelynn. 2014. "Information Prescriptions, 1930–2013: An International History and Comprehensive Review." *Journal of the Medical Library Association* 102, no. 4 (October): 271–80. doi: http://dx.doi.org/10.3163/1536-5050.102.4.008.

NN/LM (National Network of Libraries of Medicine). 2015. "About the New England Region." National Network of Libraries of Medicine, New England Region. Accessed September 4. https://nnlm.gov/ner/about.

Olney, Cynthia A., and Susan J. Barnes. 2013. *Getting Started with Community-Based Outreach, Booklets 1, 2, and 3.* 2nd ed. Seattle, WA: National Network of Libraries of Medicine, Outreach Evaluation Resource Center.

Rubin, Rhea Joyce. 2001. *Planning for Library Services to People with Disabilities.* Chicago: Association of Specialized and Cooperative Library Agencies.

Smith, Sarah, and Mark Duman. 2009. "The State of Consumer Health Information: An Overview." *Health Information & Libraries Journal* 26, no. 4 (December): 260–78. doi:10.1.1111/j.1471-1842.2009.00870.x.

Swan, D. W., J. Grimes, T. Owens, et al. 2014. *Public Libraries in the United States Survey, Fiscal Year 2012.* (IMLS-2015-PLS-01). Washington, DC: Institute of Museum and Library Services. http://www.imls.gov/research/public_libraries_in_the_us_fy_2012_report.aspx.

Tennant, Michele R. 2014. "Outreach Services in Health Sciences Libraries." In *Health Sciences Librarianship*, edited by M. Sandra Wood, 226–51. Lanham, MD: Rowman and Littlefield.

Verité Healthcare Consultants. 2013. *Community Health Needs Assessment Prepared for Baystate Medical Center.* Alexandria, VA: Verité Healthcare Consultants, LLC.

## 7

Consumer Health and the Department of Veterans Affairs Library Network

Priscilla L. Stephenson, *Corporal Michael J. Crescenz VA Medical Center, Philadelphia*; Teresa R. Coady, *Orlando VA Medical Center*; Diane K. Kromke, *Louis Stokes Cleveland VA Medical Center*; Laurie A. Barnett, *James A. Haley VA Veterans' Hospital, Tampa*; Cornelia E. Camerer, *North Florida/South Georgia Veterans Health System, Gainesville*

Consumer health practices across the Department of Veterans Affairs (VA) Library Network (VALNET) are as diverse as the VA medical centers they serve. While VALNET librarians play a critical role in patient care by delivering current, knowledge-based information to VA clinical staff, VALNET has a long tradition of providing services and resources directly to veterans in support of patient education. Although consumer health focuses on the provision of health information for the lay person, the librarians in the VA have broadened that scope to encompass many services that enhance the veteran's quality of life, such as computer instruction, support for employment efforts, or locating information about housing opportunities.

This chapter begins with brief program descriptions demonstrating best practices evident in several VA libraries. Two case studies follow with more in-depth information about specific VA library programs. The first describes how an existing hospital library service was revamped to become a multifaceted veteran-centric library program. A second case study describes how a hospital library delivers packets of focused medical information to inpatients explaining their medical conditions. The chapter concludes with a summary of VALNET best practices.

EXAMPLES OF VALNET BEST PRACTICES IN CONSUMER HEALTH

The VA has implemented the concept of patient-centered care (PCC) that focuses on empowering veterans to define and achieve lifelong health and well-being goals. Many librarians are serving on local PCC teams to assist in the delivery of consumer health information to patients and staff. Below are examples of best practices that have been implemented by librarians at one or more VA medical centers.

Information Prescriptions

The libraries at several VA medical centers provide health information to fill "information prescriptions." During the patient's clinical visit, the provider can "prescribe" that the patient go to the library for information regarding a specific diagnosis, medication, or related health issues. The written prescription can be embedded into the electronic patient record, arriving as an electronic consult to the librarian, or a printed information prescription pad can be used. The librarian "fills" the prescription with a tailored packet created to meet the specifications of the provider and the needs of the patient. When prescriptions are received electronically, the request form allows the questioner to indicate a preferred delivery method (pickup, snail mail, or secure messaging). The librarian can document the encounter in the electronic medical record, noting what information was given to the patient and adding any comments or questions that arose during the interview. For some libraries this is a new service, but the Battle Creek, Michigan, VA library, for example, has been filling information request consults in the electronic medical record system for twelve years.

At the James A. Haley VA Medical Center in Tampa, Florida, the Information Prescription Service is managed by the Patient Education Librarian. She visits the floors once a week to speak with the nursing staff and to visit patient rooms. The librarian collects Health Information Request forms from nurses who have requested research for themselves or for their patients. During her visits to patient rooms, the librarian distributes forms for the patients to use to request information regarding their condition(s) or other health concerns. Patients who are not in their rooms receive a "Sorry we missed you" card. Back in the library, the librarian conducts searches on a daily basis to respond to those information requests. In difficult cases, the librarian consults clinical staff prior to providing information to the patient.

Outpatient Clinics

During interdisciplinary Diabetes Wellness Clinics, the librarian serves on a team comprised of clinicians (endocrinologist, dietitian, doctor, podiatrist, optometrist, ophthalmologist, and nurse). The librarian explains online consumer health tools, shares print material, and answers any information questions that arise. In San Juan, Puerto Rico, the librarian provides health information during regularly scheduled visits to several patient clinics, including mental health, cardiology, and women's health.

Standardized Audiovisual Patient Education

It's important for medical center staff to work with standard protocols for various conditions and procedures. VALNET librarians work with nurse educators to provide patient education materials that can be delivered at the bedside or in the library. In Shreveport, Louisiana, nurses can request material from a list of library DVDs to help inform specific patients about their health condition. Librarians ensure that the video and equipment are brought to the bedside of patients unable to come to the library. The program standardizes patient education in that nurses are aware of exactly what information was covered with the patient, and it familiarizes ambulatory patients with the library and its resources. This popular program has resulted in patients returning to the library on their follow-up clinic visits. In Battle Creek, Michigan, the library provides DVD programs for the in-house closed-circuit television system for patients to view from their hospital rooms. In Cleveland the library records requested health information on CDs for low-vision patients.

Spanish Outreach

The North Florida/South Georgia Veterans Health System has made a special effort to reach out to the many Spanish-speaking veterans who use its medical centers in Lake City and Gainesville. The patient libraries in each location have a combined collection of some forty-five hundred books, of which twelve hundred are consumer health titles. Much of this collection is in Spanish to better serve the large Spanish-speaking population of the area. Titles are selected by a librarian and a native Spanish speaker.

The Gainesville and Lake City patient libraries have other Spanish-language consumer health resources, including pamphlets, magazines, and DVDs. They also subscribe to a number of recreational magazines and leisure reading titles in Spanish. For the Spanish readers in these medical centers, the collections in these patient libraries support patient-centered care and help to promote healthy lifestyles in a large segment of the population.

Stroke Patient Book Club

Veterans with aphasia (language disorder) and alexia (reading disorder) have challenges connecting the written work with the spoken word. At the James A. Haley VA Medical Center in Tampa, the patient librarian collaborates with speech pathologists to support their work. The librarian loads book titles onto pairs of Kindles and MP3 players, using identical visual and audio versions of each title. Each participating veteran "reads" the Kindle while listening to the audio version, completes "homework" questions about plot and vocabulary, and participates in weekly group discussions. The program reports great success in helping patients to once again link the written and spoken word, increasing their understanding of what they see and hear and helping those with speech problems to regain vocal skills.

Computer and Information Literacy

Many veterans lack up-to-date computer skills, due either to lack of access to computers or lack of access to training. For VALNET libraries that have the space, equipment, and staff, computer training has proven to be a popular way to support the VA's emphasis on patient-centered care. In Philadelphia, a volunteer provides weekly one-on-one tutorial sessions to outpatients, teaching them basic keyboard skills, e-mail use, file management, or whatever training the veteran requests (see figure 7.1). As a retired high school math teacher, the volunteer trainer has the skills of both a teacher and computer user, and his sessions have proved to be incredibly popular and successful. He is often called on to assist with veterans creating resumés or filing applications on USAjobs.gov.

Figure 7.1. Photograph of computer trainer

The VA has two major online programs of interest to many veterans—My Health*e*Vet and eBenefits. Veterans can access their personal health records on My Health*e*Vet, and eBenefits provides access to their compensation and pension claims. Many of the VALNET libraries provide assistance for veterans learning to access these systems, which can be intimidating to those without prior computer experience. Currently, twelve VALNET libraries provide computer training opportunities, and five report that they provide instruction on job search skills and resumé development. At the library in Alexandria, Louisiana, the library also provides instruction on using Louisiana's state job search website and the Supplemental Nutrition Assistance Program (SNAP) for food stamp applicants. The patient library at the Tampa VA provides access to a commercial database designed to help job seekers learn about resumé development, interview skills, and other valuable job search skills.

Providing computer access and training also creates the opportunity to teach patients about MedlinePlus and other noncommercial Internet health information websites. Access to online computer health information improves understanding and participation in treatment and wellness goals. Experience with locating any type of information using the Internet benefits patients by putting into their hands the ability to learn and grow across a range of life issues that impact their well-being: employment, educational, and housing opportunities; downloading essential documents and forms; banking; personal communication; and entertainment or hobbies.

Social Networking Support

For some veterans therapy can involve providing opportunities for camaraderie with other veterans and the community. A number of VA medical centers have innovative programs using art, music, gardening, and writing to help veterans. At the VA New York Harbor Healthcare System, the librarian worked with the mental health recovery coordinator to create a juried art show showcasing the work of the Veterans Coalition for the Arts, a program of the New York School of Visual Arts. The event was featured on New York Harbor's Facebook page (https://www.facebook.com/notes/va-ny-harbor-healthcare-system/camaraderie/995813897099324).

VALNET libraries offer a variety of other approaches in support of the patient care programs in their medical centers. In Walla Walla, Washington, the librarian helped organize a popular book club for behavioral health patients. The library provides a meeting place for the group, as well as support for book selection. In Tampa, the patient library has purchased a commercial database about gardening to support the medical center's Master Gardener program organized for the veterans.

Recreational Reading Collections

Outpatients at VA medical centers often have multiple appointments on a given day, and for many, a visit to the library helps pass the time between appointments. Several VALNET libraries have developed recreational reading collections to provide these patients with a welcome break. These libraries provide veterans with magazines, newspapers, and books—often in both print and electronic formats. At the North Florida/South Georgia Veterans Health System, the patient library has added a collection of recorded electronic audio books, as well as CDs and DVD titles. The collection there also boasts large-print titles that are popular with senior citizens, both because of the enlarged font and also because these books are often lighter weight and easier for older hands to hold. In Chillicothe, Ohio, and Philadelphia, the VA libraries use donated books for their leisure reading collections, and veterans are free to take the books with them if they wish.

Ward Carts

By far the most common activity among VALNET libraries is the use of ward carts for delivery of leisure reading materials such as books or newspapers to inpatients as well as nursing home residents. In some locations, these reading carts are linked to the library's information prescription service, so that the librarian can offer health information services while delivering magazines and books to the patients. In Shreveport, volunteers use carts to distribute magazines and donated paperbacks to in-patient rooms on a weekly basis.

Planetree Model

Several VALNET libraries have renovated their existing spaces by adopting facets of the Planetree model in order to bring a more humanistic approach to health care. They have attempted to create improved learning spaces for veterans. Improvements vary depending on the needs of the population of the particular medical center, but all have been devised to create a responsive and welcoming environment for learning to take place. At the Philadelphia VA medical center, a recent renovation removed excess shelving no longer needed due to the growth of the electronic journal collection. The result is a library that is more open and welcoming, and one that attracts increasing numbers of visitors—both veterans and medical center staff. Additional space for patient computers has meant that there is room for instruction at each computer, and wheelchair visitors find their approach to the computers unhindered. A large open space provides room for soft lounge chairs surrounded by low shelving housing the library's reference collection.

In Sheridan, Wyoming, the updated patient library includes a new collection of large-print books and an audiobook collection. These resources helped to provide new recreational reading for domiciliary and other patients in this facility. The renovation of the Sheridan VA's patient library was so successful that the librarian and her supervisor were invited to present at the 2011 Planetree conference about the transformation of the library into a veteran-centered oasis.

CASE STUDY: ESTABLISHING A NEW PROGRAM
AT ORLANDO VA MEDICAL CENTER LIBRARY

Prior to 1975, veterans in central Florida who required medical treatment had options for service at the Naval Hospital in Orlando or they could travel to Tampa, Bay Pines, or other affiliated VAs. In 1975, the Orlando VA Outpatient Clinic and Assistance Office opened, later to become the Orlando VA Medical Center. For years, the library served both patients and medical staff in the same physical space. In 2013, a new library director evaluated how the space was being used and completed a needs assessment to determine how veterans could better be served. No delineation existed to separate the patient resources from the medical, and veterans and patients intermingled chaotically. As services and resources for veterans were reviewed, it became apparent that changes were required to reorganize the limited space into two distinct sections, one clearly for veterans, and the other for medical staff.

The section for veterans evolved into a patient-centered library that addresses veterans' information needs. Library staff desks were moved to a prominent point of service, with the station visible upon entry into the library, and all nonessential desks and items were removed. New furniture was ordered to help reconfigure the library. This space included a dedicated veteran computer lab, where three new computers brought the total to five. One computer provides dedicated access to the VA's online personal health record, My HealtheVet (MHV). The online portal provides opportunities for veterans to make informed decisions and manage their health care by partnering with their health care teams. Library staff assist veterans with registration and authentication, and teach them how to navigate its many features, such as how to send secure messages to communicate with health care providers; how to search for medication information; how to refill prescriptions; how to make requests for appointments; and how to review laboratory test results. MHV also hosts the Veterans Health Library (VHL), an online tool for locating patient health education information.

Four computers were configured with unique desktop icons to address veterans' specific health questions or life issues. Icons include MHV, MedlinePlus, eBenefits, USAJobs, Social Security, National Archives, VA for Vets, Food Stamps, Google, Word, and Excel. To further assist veterans in exploring career interests, building employment skills, constructing resumés, and practicing interview questions, the library purchased an online career transition database and made it available to veterans in the library and also remotely. Veterans use the computer lab to locate consumer health information, seek employment, check personal e-mail, connect with support groups, and create documents and spreadsheets. Library staff also offer professional searches of sites such as MedlinePlus or the VHL and print the information for veterans.

Partnering with local libraries has proved beneficial to reach veterans who otherwise might not know about information services available through the VA. The Orlando VA library and the Orlando Public Library are creating a veteran-centered webpage to be accessible from both libraries' websites. The LibGuide site is in development and will feature library services and resources relevant to veterans' needs, such as health information, computer classes, databases that would be useful for writing resumes, DIY (do it yourself) technology classes, booklists, and access to the Melrose Technology Camps (hands-on training provided by the county library system for subjects such as the digital arts, science, technology, engineering, and math).

The library's needs assessment in 2013 also revealed that the physical collection lacked adequate resources to meet the needs of the veteran population. There were no patient education books, no magazines or newspapers, no audiovisuals, and no recreational reading material. The librarian developed a new veteran and consumer health collection using standard book recommendation lists and comparative analysis of collections in other VA libraries for medical centers of similar size and scope.

Informal conversations with veterans visiting the library helped to further define material that would be beneficial to their information needs. As the new collection grew, the material was housed in the veterans' section of the library, separate from the medical staff collection. The new core collection of consumer health books included topics such as mental health, women's health, drug information, caregiving, diseases, health and wellness, self-help, and military health.

Based on veteran requests, the library purchased subscriptions to over one hundred magazine titles. Titles include consumer health magazines such as *Healthy Living* and the *Mayo Clinic Health Letter*, as well as popular reading magazines such as *National Geographic*, *Southern Living*, and *U.S. News & World Report*. The library also subscribes to four newspapers—the *Orlando Sentinel*, *USA Today*, the *Wall Street Journal*, and the *New York Times*.

The library purchased a collection of audio books with CD and MP3 formats with subject matter consisting of health and self-improvement topics. Topics range from guides for reducing stress to guides for healthy eating and special diets. Because music can help regulate patient stress and encourage relaxation, the library added a collection of CDs featuring rock, jazz, piano, classical, reggae, pop, folk, rhythm and blues, instrumental, opera, easy listening, and country music. Patients can check out consumer health books, movie or music DVDs, and audio books for three-week periods. Residents at the affiliated VA Lake Nona Domiciliary have no direct access to the Orlando facility, so the library has placed a second collection of gently used donated books on permanent loan at that location. Many of the titles have been donated by two nonprofit organizations that regularly donate books for veterans.

The library director also serves an important role on the medical center's Health Education Committee, an interdisciplinary committee that meets monthly to review and approve all in-house patient health education flyers and brochures. This group verifies the accuracy of content, checks to ensure appropriate reading level, and ensures easy-to-read format. Examples of document titles are the "Sleep Questionnaire," "Warfarin Anti-Coagulation Data Form," and a letter "Congratulations on Your Pregnancy."

The interaction between the library staff and the patrons has grown and strengthened as they assist veterans with web and printed resources, provide help with the computers, and respond to requests for health information. Now health care providers routinely send veterans to the library for health information relating to their specific diagnoses, treatments, or medications.

To gather comments and suggestions, the library has a suggestion form that veterans can use to recommend new projects and make requests for services and resources. The library staff uses these suggestions to help determine future directions for library services. In addition, the library markets its services and resources with colorful red, white, and blue flyers posted throughout the facility. Feedback from veterans has been positive, indicating that the library provides them with services they value and use frequently. The importance of having friendly, helpful staff can never be underestimated. A veteran library customer recently remarked, "Thank you for placing a patient, gentle, and knowledgeable professional in the library. The librarian certainly provides much needed on-the-spot help to those of us who served and are now physically wounded."

As any library director has discovered when beginning at a new facility, the challenges often seem overwhelming. But it is also exciting to face the opportunity to improve upon existing services and resources that can impact the information needs and learning of the library's patron base. As shown in this case study, the Orlando VA Medical Center Library presented many opportunities for improvement, but the vision existed within the medical center to build a library program that would be worthy of the new facility that was in construction at Lake Nona. Plans for the facility included space for two distinct libraries—one for patients, and one for staff. With that intention in place, the new library director in 2013 was afforded significant support and leeway in implementing changes and improvements in space, staff size, collection, resources, and technology. However, changes are always evaluated based on their successful implementation, and those instituted at the Orlando VA Medical Center library proved to be of value to both veterans and staff alike.

CASE STUDY: PERC PACKS

In the Louis Stokes Cleveland VA Medical Center in Cleveland, Ohio, the library also manages a Patient Education Resource Center, or PERC. The library staff there has worked with interdisciplinary teams consisting of patient educators, nurse educators, dietitians, and physicians to develop a unique approach to patient education for inpatients. They have developed a series of educational packets called PERC Packs. The librarian at the PERC coordinates the creation and delivery of the packets.

When a veteran is admitted to the medical center, the educators take advantage of the opportunity to provide relevant health education regarding the patient's condition and any prescribed medications or treatments. The primary goal of PERC Packs is to help reduce re-admission rates and emergency room visits by educating patients and their families to recognize and treat signs and symptoms before they become severe enough to require inpatient stays or emergency room visits. Both the patient and the medical center benefit when patients are healthier and treatment costs are reduced.

Consistency in the information provided by the various departments of the medical center is important. PERC Packs standardize information given to the patients, no matter where the education is given or who the educator may be. For patients with visual impairment, PERC Packs can be printed in larger type sizes or used with screen readers. For patients with reading difficulties, the library provides CD recordings. During accreditation surveys, various surveyors have commented favorably on the use of PERC Packs.

Each PERC Pack contains a clinician cover sheet, a patient cover sheet, and preselected patient health education material on routine topics (see figures 7.2 and 7.3). The cover sheet for staff is designed to be used as a teaching plan and tracking checklist to guide clinicians. Most PERC Packs are six to eight double-sided pages, including both cover sheets. Sources for the health information in each pack include locally created materials, reproducible materials

Patient ID: _____			Date: _____	

December 2014 revision

Diabetes Education – PERC Pack
Interdisciplinary Team** Teaching Checklist for Patient/Caregiver

Date	Nurse Providing Education	Topic	Comments
		A1C Know Your Number	
		How to Draw Up and Inject Insulin	
		Sick Day Guide	
		Hypoglycemia 15 – 15 Rule	

Date	Team Member Providing Education	Topic	Comments
		Overview of diabetes	
		Do you have Type 1 or Type 2?	
		Blood Glucose Testing	
		Do you have a meter? *[If no, alert diabetes educators]*, BG target ranges, log book	
		HgbA1c	
		Do you know your A1C "Less than 8 is great!"	
		Dietary Guidelines	
		Which foods affect your blood sugar? Are you eating scheduled meals?	
		Medications	
		Do you know what diabetes medications you are taking?	

Figure 7.2.   Clinician Cover Sheet

from other sources such as the National Institutes of Health (NIH) or the U.S. Food and Drug Administration (FDA), and information from subscribed databases such as Krames On-Demand (https://www.kramesondemand.com/Login.aspx?URL=/index.aspx&). The patient cover sheet shown in figure 7.3 explains that the information included in the PERC Pack has been requested by a member of the patient's health care team.

PERC Pack

provided by the Patient Education Resource Center

A member of your health care team has requested this handout for you. If you have any questions about your care or this health information, please talk to your doctor or other qualified healthcare provider.

You may also call a Tele-Nurse at any time at 1-888-XXX-XXXX toll free.

This handout provides a general overview on this topic and may not be specific to you. Always follow the advice of your health care team.

Figure 7.3.   Patient Cover Sheet

Initially PERC Packs were available on the topics of chronic obstructive pulmonary disease (COPD), diabetes, and heart failure. Stroke became available the second year, and hypertension followed the next year. When they order a PERC Pack, clinicians have the opportunity to request information on any other topic needed. These topics can then be used to help determine the need for future PERC Packs.

Physicians can request PERC Packs in the electronic health record as part of the admission order set, or health care staff can place the order after a patient arrives on the ward. Order requests generate a standard consult or alert sent to the PERC librarian, who then notes delivery of the PERC Pack in the electronic health record. Daily reports run against medical center admissions identify any patients with unusual readings, such as an A1C of 8 percent or higher who have not had a diabetes PERC Pack ordered for them. PERC staff deliver all requested PERC Packs to the designated contacts on each ward by 8 PM the next business day.

Evolution and Expansion

PERC Packs have been so well received that their use is expanding to the outpatient care setting as well. Although the PERC staff do not make daily deliveries to outpatient areas to fill specific requests, they maintain a supply of PERC Packs that are stored in the outpatient clinics, ready for on-demand use. The files are also available online for printing, as needed.

This has led to the creation of a new type of PERC Pack called the Special PERC Pack. Special PERC Packs are created in the same format, but they are housed in ward and clinic areas for on-demand use in both inpatient and outpatient settings, rather than daily ward delivery. Use can be triggered by reports or scores, as is the case with Smoking Cessation and Pressure Ulcer Prevention. The "Nephrostomy Tubes" PERC Pack is used solely by a small set of specially trained clinicians. Others such as "Foley Catheter Care" and "Fall Prevention" are available on demand in any clinical area.

Figure 7.4 shows that in 2014 there were a total of 2,905 PERC Packs delivered, but there were a total of 1,905 consults, indicating that many requests are for more than one PERC Pack topic. The highest number of requests were for information on diabetes and hypertension.

Some wards have begun to track usage of the PERC Packs by verifying documentation of education in the medical record. Data are compiled and presented as a graph for the five wards that receive the greatest number of PERC Packs. Figure 7.5 shows a one-month compilation of the five medical wards that routinely report PERC Pack usage. The 76 percent overall usage rate is impressive, considering that many patients are discharged only a few hours after the PERC Packs are delivered to the ward. A potential future enhancement

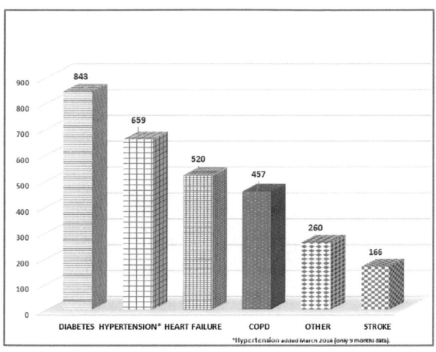

Figure 7.4. PERC Packs Requested by Topic 2014

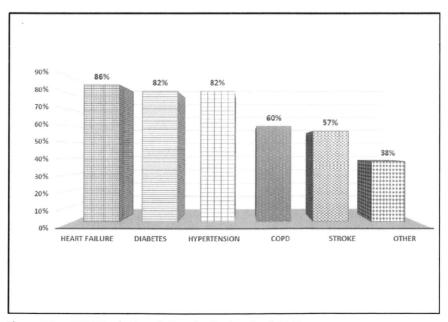

Figure 7.5. PERC Pack Completions by Topic—April 2015

would be twice daily delivery of PERC Packs, which would allow staff more time to use the materials with patients prior to discharge.

Perks for the PERC?

PERC Packs promote the visibility and professional presence of the librarian. People forget about the library if they see staff only on rare occasions, or perhaps not at all. Many librarians don't leave the library, and then wonder why more people don't come to the library for assistance with information requests. At this medical center, ward and clinic staff will look for the librarians and may stop them in the halls to ask questions about services or request information for specific patients.

We live in an era when the notion that "Everything is on the Internet, and I can just Google it" seems to prevail. Librarians need visibility and an active clinical support base within the facility. The ward and clinic contacts made with people who can be called on later for information, advice, and referrals to other employees and services will provide a better understanding of ward priorities and needs and demands on clinician time, and they can help steer you toward providing a solution that works better for patients and fellow employees. The ward clerk or unit secretary can provide friendly advice about ward and clinic functions and routines and help locate the person in charge; this is also the person most likely to answer the phone.

Projects like PERC Packs provide an opportunity to learn about how other parts of the medical center really work, and they also demonstrate how a librarian's role can expand to fill a need.

BEST PRACTICES—SUPPORTING
PATIENT-CENTERED CARE IN VALNET LIBRARIES

Veterans Health Administration medical centers provide unique opportunities for hospital librarians to expand the normal scope of library services to patients. Although VA medical centers provide surgery and other in-patient procedures, by far the largest proportion of patients use the VA's outpatient services. VA facilities support in-patient mental health services, and many have nursing homes and/or domiciliary facilities. VALNET libraries support these patient groups with a variety of programs that often present unique approaches not available to other hospital librarians.

Because VA outpatients return for clinic visits on a regular basis, veterans are available to attend developmental programs such as book clubs or computer classes that build on past training or discussions. With the VA's national directive to support a mission of patient-centered care, there is administrative support for library programming that meets patients' informational and educational needs. Computer training for veterans, in particular, is a natural task for VA librarians for whom database training is already an important role, working with employees to demonstrate PubMed and other databases. VALNET libraries have become strong supporters of the VA's electronic health record system, training veterans to use MyHealtheVet and eBenefits, in particular.

Outpatient clinics for chronic conditions, such as diabetes or asthma, provide VA librarians with unique opportunities to provide support for patient education programs, which may mean providing book and DVD listings of library materials or leading discussions of library resources during group meetings with patients and their caregivers. VA libraries provide a similar support service for hospital in-patients, with their ward cart and information prescription services, bringing needed health information materials to the bedside.

CONCLUSION

VA libraries reflect their mission of patient-centered care in a variety of ways. Whether it's developing a consumer health book collection, providing computer assistance, or delivering magazines and paperbacks to patients at the bedside, these medical centers have found unique ways to reach out to the patients in their facilities. VALNET has a long tradition of providing services and resources directly to veterans in support of patient education. Although consumer health focuses on the provision of health information for the lay person, the librarians in the VA have broadened that scope to encompass many services that enhance the veteran's quality of life, such as computer instruction, support for employment efforts, or locating information about housing opportunities.

## 8

The Learning Center

A Cancer Consumer Health Library at MD Anderson Cancer Center

ELIZABETH BRACKEEN, *The Learning Center,*
MD Anderson Cancer Center

The Learning Center is a consumer health library and the patient-facing component of Patient Education at MD Anderson Cancer Center. The library is staffed with a mix of health educators, librarians, and nurses. The Learning Center has three locations on the main campus of MD Anderson in Houston, Texas: one in each of the two outpatient clinic areas and a third in the Rotary House Hotel. Each of the three Learning Centers are open to the public but primarily serve patients and their families, staff, and visitors. The mission of the Learning Center is to enable patrons to participate fully in making informed decisions about their health care through the provision of educational resources related to health, cancer, and cancer prevention.

The main campus of MD Anderson is located within the Texas Medical Center and has both inpatient and outpatient facilities. In 2014, one hundred twenty thousand patients were seen at MD Anderson and nearly twenty-eight thousand of those had an inpatient stay. Two-thirds of the patients come from within Texas, with the majority of the remaining third coming from elsewhere in the United States. Three percent of visitors to MD Anderson are international patients. The three Learning Centers see over thirty thousand visitors annually.

ORIGIN

The consumer health information program at MD Anderson has always had its home within Patient Education, but the history of the Learning Center is shaped by cooperation among many departments within the institution.

The origin of the Learning Center in 1996 was a convergence of Patient Education, Patient Guest Relations, Cancer Prevention, the Research Medical Library, and the Development Office. This cooperative work exemplifies what is needed for a successful consumer health library in a large institution. Patient Guest Relations had the idea to start the program, and Patient Education provided the expertise in patient education resources. The Cancer Prevention Center had the budget and real estate to implement the program, and the Research Medical Library gave operational support and library expertise. Finally, the Development Office made the program possible with funding for furniture and the original collection. Without support in any of these areas, a successful and sustainable program would have been much more difficult to achieve. The most important ingredient was the personal relationships that fostered the willingness to work across departments and divisions to create the Learning Center.

FUNDING

Donations from Theodore N. Law, the Levit Family, and the Holden Foundation made it possible to get the individual Learning Centers up and running. The funding for day-to-day personnel and non-personnel expenses of the Learning Center comes directly out of the Patient Education operational budget. In fiscal year 2015–2016, the non-personnel budget for the three Learning Centers was $60,000 with $35,000 of that spent on collection development, which includes books, audiovisual and print materials, and journals.

FACILITIES

The Learning Center is allotted fifty-seven hundred square feet distributed across three different buildings. The three locations combined provide just over thirty-five hundred publicly accessible square feet. In addition to that, there are two classrooms at approximately four hundred seventy-five square feet each that also double as meeting rooms. The twelve hundred square feet that remain are office and workspace for staff and volunteers. This would be enough space if there were not a need for storage of print materials. This lack of storage has an impact on staffing in that we cannot do bulk orders. The iterative ordering throughout the year increases the staff time necessary for ordering and receiving materials.

STAFFING

Seven and one-half full-time employees staff the library's three reference desks, which are open for a combined total of ninety hours per week. Two full-service locations are each staffed thirty-five hours per week and one self-service location is staffed twenty hours per week. In addition to full- and part-time staff, seven to ten volunteers provide an additional thirty to forty hours of service per week. Each location has a volunteer liaison responsible for communications and training of the Learning Center volunteers. Volunteer Services at MD Anderson Cancer Center is a centralized institutional program. Throughout the institution there are approximately twelve hundred volunteers in a variety of roles that provide over one hundred thousand hours of service annually. The Learning Center works with volunteer coordinators to match people with jobs that suit their interests and skills. The Learning Center needs volunteers who are happy to do the sometimes tedious work demanded of a library setting. Volunteers spend most of their time helping with the distribution of print materials both within the library and in the outpatient clinics and with processing incoming books, CDs, and DVDs. In addition, they assist with shelving, shelf reading, and gathering data on the distribution of materials for a monthly report.

DATA COLLECTION

Tracking usage numbers and figuring out the impact of the Learning Center is an effort that continues to evolve over time. From hash marks on a sheet of paper, to people counters on the doors, to electronic forms, the Learning Center's impact is measured in a number of ways. In the two full-service locations, desk staff manually counts the number of people through the door. These locations did have door counters for a number of years, but they proved to be quite inaccurate. The Holden Learning Center in the Rotary House Hotel is self-service for the majority of the hours it is opened, so even though it is inaccurate, a door counter is the only way to measure usage. In addition to the number of people that come in, e-mail, and call, staff also tracks the number of minutes (or hours) spent with individual patrons. Additional data are collected (see figure 8.1), such as whether the patron is a patient or a staff member, what type of cancer is involved, topics the patron is interested in, and where else within and outside of the institution the patron is referred to. Time spent with patients and staff is also accounted for.

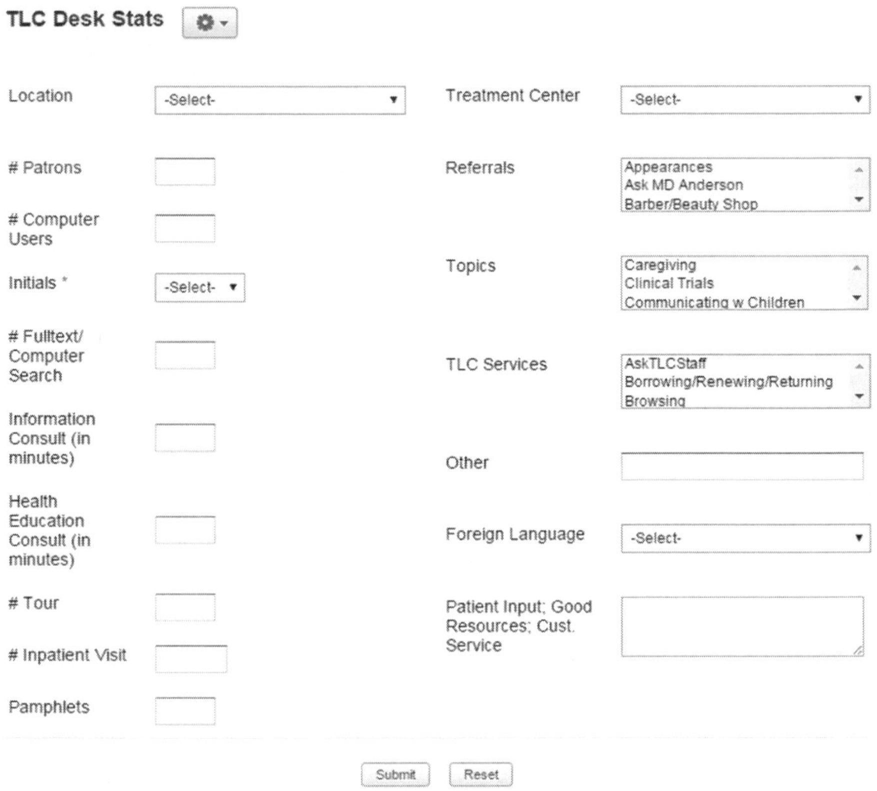

TLC Desk Stats ⚙▾

Location	-Select- ▾	Treatment Center	-Select- ▾
# Patrons	☐	Referrals	Appearances / Ask MD Anderson / Barber/Beauty Shop
# Computer Users	☐		
Initials *	-Select- ▾	Topics	Caregiving / Clinical Trials / Communicating w Children
# Fulltext/ Computer Search	☐	TLC Services	AskTLCStaff / Borrowing/Renewing/Returning / Browsing
Information Consult (in minutes)	☐	Other	☐
Health Education Consult (in minutes)	☐	Foreign Language	-Select- ▾
# Tour	☐	Patient Input; Good Resources; Cust. Service	☐
# Inpatient Visit	☐		
Pamphlets	☐		

[Submit]   [Reset]

Figure 8.1. Web form to collect desk statistics

Nowadays, it is easy to create a web-accessible form to track any kind of data the organization deems of interest. When departmental or institutional initiatives need to be tracked, an electronic web-based form allows the flexibility of change that is accessible immediately by all staff. If staff are diligent in their data-entry, the reporting from this kind of system can be very informative. Data can point to patient populations that are underutilizing the Learning Center, and outreach and programming can be planned for the clinical staff in those areas. At the end of each fiscal year, this form is reviewed to remove the data points that are no longer relevant and to add any new programs or services that need to be tracked. On a technical note, even though there is limited storage, implementation in Zoho Creator was selected over Google Forms because of Creator's ability to display columns, which Google Forms does not support. Being able to see the entire form on the screen increases the quality of the data collected by staff.

PATIENT FEEDBACK

Getting patient feedback can be difficult in a large hospital environment where the amount of paperwork and surveying patients' experience is already onerous. The Learning Center has almost continuously collected customer satisfaction data. Originally, paper surveys were given to patients as they visited Learning Center locations. That effort expanded to placing a survey inside borrowed books for patrons to complete prior to returning. A transition from fully paper surveys to fully electronic surveys has taken place over the last decade, and the results have been uniformly positive. The questions on the survey have been worked and reworked to elicit constructive feedback, but they consistently report back only high levels of satisfaction and gratitude. It has been difficult to get constructive criticism out of grateful patrons. The latest effort has been a focus on patient feedback on specific materials rather than service so that patients are not asked to be critical of the individual helping them. In a recent project, staff printed Post-it notes with a survey URL in a selection of nutrition pamphlets to get feedback on the materials, but the return rate was very low. Collecting data from one-on-one conversations with patrons is time consuming, but remains the most effective method for obtaining feedback from patients by Learning Center staff.

PUBLIC SERVICES

The Learning Center, as the patient-facing component of Patient Education, offers both library and business services. For patients and families in the hospital, full service reference is available at two locations for seven hours a day, five days per week. For guests of the Rotary House, self-service access to the Holden Learning Center is available seven days per week, including evening hours. Rotary House guests have access to desk staff both in person on weekday mornings and via the Reference Request form. The Reference Request form is written specifically for the oncology setting. The form asks questions regarding the cancer diagnosis including cell type, sites of primary and secondary cancers, and stage. The form works well for patients conversant in their diagnosis, but it is likely intimidating for those not familiar with the terminology of cancer.

Customer Service

Learning Center staff strive to provide the highest level of customer service to anyone who walks in the door, e-mails, or calls. Each person is greeted and offered assistance when they arrive. If they are new to MD Anderson, staff will ask whether they have visited the Learning Center before. If not, they are given a brief overview of services. When patients and family members visit, staff take extra care to listen carefully to what they are saying, how they are saying it, and what they are not saying. Staff listen for clues about current knowledge, reading level, and familiarity with their disease or treatment. Asking clarifying questions without leading the conversation is important. Some subject knowledge can be helpful when discussing a cancer diagnosis. An instructive example in oncology is cancer of the tongue. When a patient or family member comes in asking for information on tongue cancer, the American Cancer Society and the National Cancer Institute websites are great places to start for general information. But, neither include tongue cancer in their A-to-Z lists. Depending where on the tongue the cancer is located, tongue cancer may be diagnosed as either oropharyngeal or hypopharyngeal cancer. So, "Is your cancer on the front of the tongue or the base of the tongue?" is the very first clarifying question a librarian trying to help a tongue cancer patient needs to know to ask. Each type of cancer has its own unique clarifying questions, and it takes time to obtain that knowledge. Two strategies for handling a consumer cancer reference interview when one is unfamiliar with the topic are: (1) "I have not had the opportunity to research this type of cancer before but I know some great places to get us started" or (2) "Did your doctor give you an exact diagnosis and staging?" In scenario one, the patient and librarian learn together as they go. In scenario two, the answer is often "No" and the patient has to go back to the clinic or consult their electronic health record to get the answer. It is important to answer the questions that patrons ask and not direct the conversation into subject areas that they are unfamiliar or uncomfortable with. Ideally the conversation leads the patrons to materials and information that can help them ask better questions of their health care team.

Reference Services

Reference services in the Learning Center comprise face-to-face, e-mail, and telephone reference. Patients and family members who visit in person take priority, but the Learning Centers are open to the general public, and library staff will assist anyone who arrives, calls, or e-mails to the best of their ability. Generally there is one staff member on the desk at a time with others in offices close by who are available when assistance is needed. There is often a volunteer who can help with triage and directional questions when the desk gets hectic. If a patron does not have time to wait to be helped, staff provide them either access to the e-mail reference service or with a paper Reference

Request form to complete. Staff then follow up with them via mail, e-mail, or over the phone. When e-mail and telephone reference questions come from patrons who are not current patients, staff often refer them to online resources or similar services in their area. The questions asked by patrons range widely. Some common examples are how to eat right, how to make a decision about treatment, and how to find literature to dispute a denied insurance claim.

Circulation Services

The doors of the Learning Center are open to the general public, and the circulating collection is as well. These libraries are located within a very large institution, which is situated within the largest medical center in the world. The physical location and the price of parking in this area of the city allow for this open-door policy. In a more publicly accessible location, staff would not be able to handle the impact of the general public and still maintain the current level of service for the patrons who are already in the building as patients, caregivers, or staff. From its earliest days, the Learning Center has circulated materials outside of the hospital. Postage-paid envelopes are offered to anyone borrowing books or audiovisual materials. The value of this expenditure is twofold—the circulating collection is more often in the hands of patrons and the library material loss rate is kept to a minimum. Considerable staff time is spent processing overdues and fines and fees notices. The Learning Center uses the Voyager ILS, which is a very sophisticated system for such a small library. Use of Voyager is made possible by the cooperative relationship the Learning Center has with the MD Anderson Research Medical Library. The Learning Center staff uses the Voyager Circulation (including a web-based public interface), Cataloging, and Reporting modules to manage the collection and circulation. Acquisitions and serials are handled in a much more rudimentary way, with spreadsheets.

Inpatient Delivery

The Learning Center staff deliver print materials and books for checkout to the inpatient areas by request. Occasionally patients call down for items, but more often, clinical staff or faculty with a book recommendation will ask for the item to be brought to the room. When delivering materials to an inpatient room, Learning Center staff give a brief overview of services with an accompanying pamphlet and bookmark. The item requested and a prepaid postage envelope are delivered. The only action required by the patient or family member is to complete our registration form. The demand for this service is manageable; usually whoever is not staffing the desk delivers the item up to the floor.

Public Computers

Between the three Learning Center locations, there are fourteen public computers available for patrons. Prior to the installation of an institution-wide wireless network for patients and guests and the proliferation of portable computers, phones, and tablets, the Learning Center had a policy that its public computers were primarily for health and medical research. If all the computers were occupied and a patron was using a computer for recreational purposes, they would be asked to temporarily make way for more urgent business. This policy has evolved with the times; due to up-grading of the MD Anderson guest wireless network and the fact that the majority of visitors bring their own devices, there is almost always a computer available. The current policy still states that "The computers in The Learning Center are primarily intended for health research purposes" and that "children under the age of sixteen must be accompanied by an adult." This policy is mostly enforced to limit staff use of computers, so that the machines are available when there is a patient need.

Technology Assistance

More than one-third of MD Anderson patients are from out of town and have a need to take care of their personal, work, and school-related business while they are in Houston. The Learning Centers provide computers with Internet and MS Office, printing, faxing, copying, and scanning free to all patients and family members. It is important for everyone on staff to be able to do rudimentary troubleshooting on the most common software and devices. Visitors most often need help accessing the guest wireless network, setting up access to their patient portal, and understanding how to access their e-mail when they are away from their home computer. Though the Learning Center mission is the provision of cancer-related resources, helping with technical problems and business services ensures that the practical needs of patients do not get in the way of them getting the best care they can.

COLLECTION DEVELOPMENT

Early in the Learning Center history, the collection development policy included a requirement to have all newly acquired items reviewed and ap-proved by clinical staff. This policy failed and was quickly changed due to the time constraints of clinical staff and the need to have materials on the shelf. Briefly, current policy is "to supply current, authoritative health information." Recommendations are regularly elicited from clinical staff in every position and specialty. Resource recommendations are also encouraged and welcomed from patrons via a form on the Learning Center website. The Learning Center is committed to providing a comprehensive English-language cancer consumer health collection. If there is a consumer health book on any type of cancer or cancer topic, the Learning Center at MD Anderson will have it on the shelf, as long as it is not making outrageous claims or recommending treatment that is not backed up by medical evidence. Self-published works are included in the collection when they are an individual patient's story and do not include recommendations for specific treatment. In the rarer types of cancer, there are so few patient stories that it can be isolating. It is worth the sacrifice of not having well-edited material so that there is something on the shelf in which a patient can see him- or herself. In addition to oncology, other subject areas in which materials are broadly collected are nutrition, cookbooks, mind-body, meditation, exercise, end-of-life, and diabetes.

Collection

The Learning Center collection focuses mainly on the continuum of cancer care, which includes prevention, detection, diagnosis, treatment, and recovery. Additional areas of focus include nutrition and integrative medicine. The cancer collection is supplemented with core works on common health and disease topics such as obesity, diabetes, heart disease, and osteoporosis. The audiovisual collection has a slightly different focus, due to a lack of audio and video published on the topic of cancer. The video collection is made up of primarily patient education self-care and supplemented with exercise videos. The audio collection is primarily focused on meditation, relaxation, humor, and current health-related audiobooks. The Learning Center continues to subscribe to a small number of periodicals. These tend to be cancer and health newsletters as well as clinical and trade publications. The most popular of all our materials is a slat wall full of over one hundred printed booklets and brochures (see figure 8.2). Though the bulk of these materials come from MD Anderson, the National Cancer Institute (NCI), the American Cancer Society, the National Comprehensive Cancer Network (NCCN), and the American Institute of Cancer Research, the library carries more than four hundred titles from over fifty organizations. In recent years, there has been a significant decrease in the availability of print materials specifically from the NCI and the NCCN, but the demand for these materials has not decreased. When patients want to pick up something to share or read in the waiting room, the vast majority prefer the printed version. This has greatly increased the amount of in-house printing of materials, which results in an increase in the cost of printing supplies as well as staff and volunteer time.

Figure 8.2. Levit Learning Center slat wall

QR Codes

Materials no longer available in print are often made available online and are often available in a format suitable for downloading and printing. For the Learning Center, the cost of printing has definitely exceeded the amount formerly budgeted for shipping and handling of the same. The Learning Center began a two-year project to test two hypotheses. One, to find out if the QR codes would be adopted by smartphone and tablet users, and two, to see if labeling all print materials with QR codes would decrease the amount of print materials being distributed. At the end of two years, it was determined that the maintenance of hundreds of QR codes, Bitly links, and thumbnail images was too much additional work for the small amount of usage the QR codes received. Even though there has been an increase in the usage of online material, that increase was not seen using QR codes physically present in the Learning Center, and there was not a decrease in the demand for print copies. The project was abandoned after two years, but one side benefit of having QR codes and Bitly links for all of the print material was a three-ring binder with all of the thumbnail images and QR codes that acted as a virtual slat wall at conferences and health fairs.

OUTREACH AND MARKETING

One of the greatest challenges the Learning Center faces is visibility within MD Anderson. The Learning Center is constantly marketing to staff. With over twenty-one thousand employees, there are new staff starting every week, and the Learning Center uses a multipronged approach to make sure they know about this library for patients and their families. Staff participate in every available institutional, divisional, and departmental event in order to promote the Learning Center Services. Staff members teach classes, give talks, present posters, staff health and awareness fairs, and staff tables to patient-facing conferences. Whenever new staff wander into the library to have a look around, we make a special effort to introduce them to the Learning Center's collection and services. It is important for Learning Center staff to understand their role, what clinic or department they are coming from and to ask how we might work together. Specifically, if there are patient materials that new clinical staff will be recommending, the Learning Center wants to have those materials available for patients. New employees often need referrals to other departments and services.

New Employee Scavenger Hunt

The Learning Center encourages directors to send their new hires for a scavenger hunt or at least for a tour. The scavenger hunts are tailored to individual areas or departments so that the new employees can be aware of the resources that their patients most commonly request. After an orientation and tour, the scavenger hunt requires new staff to browse around and identify relevant pamphlets, books, audios, videos, and recommended websites.

Health Fairs, Conferences, and Awareness Events

When MD Anderson or a local advocacy organization hosts a patient-facing conference or event, the Learning Center staff fill up a rolling cart with a table cover and relevant books, audios, and videos as well as print materials, brochures, and bookmarks. Staff take the opportunity to talk to patients and family members, staff from other MD Anderson departments, vendors, and clinical staff. Patients are always appreciative of the resources provided, but one of the greatest benefits is educating faculty and clinical staff about the available patient-facing materials and services. It is always a pleasure to see a faculty member pick up a library book from the table and say, "You have this? I recommend this to my patients all the time." Where staff then love to respond, "Yes, and we have the audiobook too."

CONTENT CREATION

Pathfinders

The staff of the Learning Center has created, and maintains annually, approximately thirty pathfinders. Pathfinders are resource guides on types of cancer, and cancer-related topics that point users to the best available books, pamphlets, audios, videos, and websites for a given topic. They are localized in that they have the Learning Center's call numbers included for the convenience of patients and staff who visit in person, and they refer to resources created by MD Anderson Patient Education that may or may not be available on the web. Currently, pathfinders are provided on paper and electronically as PDFs at http://www.mdanderson.org/tlc. This method of delivery has been discussed among staff; in the current environment with a push or pull to put everything online, the Learning Center has been unable to let go of the paper or printable version of this resource in favor of something like LibGuides. The majority of patients and caregivers who come in person to the library are not very interested in electronic delivery of health information. Because of the demand for print copies of pathfinders and staff hesitance to maintain multiple current versions of this content, these remain in an increasingly old and not mobile-friendly format. Pathfinders have been the Learning Center's greatest intra-institutional success. In addition to being available on the Learning Center site, this content has been integrated throughout the MD Anderson institutional website as additional resources for patients on all of the cancer and cancer topic-specific pages.

Podcasts

In order to have current content on the Learning Center website, staff decided to post monthly podcasts that feature a review of a pamphlet, book, audio, or video from the collection. A production schedule was created, and individual staff selected the material they would review. A communications plan was put in place for the changes to the structure of the website and the regular posting of additional content. Prior to recording, staff members write up their review and practice saying it aloud to measure the running time and make any edits. The final review podcasts are no more the four minutes long. For the visuals, each recording uses a PowerPoint template that includes the title, author, cover image of the reviewed material, a photograph and name of the staff member, and a link to the material if it is available online. The Learning Center uses an institutional license to Camtasia Relay to record the podcasts. Camtasia has the benefit of being very easy to use but only has rudimentary editing capabilities. This lack of functionality can be frustrating, as recordings have to be captured in one take. Technically, it is straightforward to record and make available podcasts on the Learning Center website; the most challenging aspect of this project is creating recordings with good enough sound quality in a noisy office environment. A good USB microphone helped, but a makeshift sound booth of packing foam really makes a noticeable improvement in the sound quality of the recording. The institutional web-analytics package allows for tracking the monthly usage of these podcasts and the data collected have been instructive. Website visitors are likely to click on disease-specific resources and even more likely to click through when information on a particular disease is scarce. Web traffic did not increase significantly, but staff will continue the podcast review program. The benefits are a growing collection of material reviews that provide unique and original content for the website.

ASSESSMENT

MD Anderson is an organization that strives for continuous improvement, and the Learning Center participates in institutional, divisional, and departmental initiatives to improve the patient experience as well as increase efficiency and effectiveness. In order to get feedback from patrons, Learning Center staff have regularly gathered customer satisfaction data using first a paper and now an electronic survey. Patrons that provide an e-mail address in their Learning Center registration are e-mailed an electronic survey through Qualtrics. The feedback received from surveys returned during the last eleven years is overwhelmingly grateful and positive and includes almost no constructive criticism. This in no way indicates that there are not areas for improvement. It is difficult to get the users of a cancer consumer library to think about what, in their experience, might be improved upon at the time that they are in need of cancer consumer library services.

A recent departmental initiative gathers specific patient feedback on patient education programs and materials. Staff documented the feedback and noted what impact this feedback might have on programs and materials. While this method is time consuming and subjective, it did provide the department with specific patient feedback that informed collection development, influenced the materials design, and improved the staff's knowledge of the collection. Individual classes and programs are assessed with satisfaction surveys, but like the data from the Learning Center satisfaction survey, there is a very high degree of satisfaction among class and program attendees.

BEST PRACTICES

In any public-facing, service-oriented operation, there are three critical elements to balance when striving for excellence. First, there is continuous improvement; from a large and bureaucratic organization to a one-person shop, there are always areas to improve. Sometimes those improvements look like multiyear projects and sometimes they look like rearranging a form so it is easier for patrons to use. Patron feedback, the second element, feeds directly into the first. Feedback can come from formal interactions like surveys or focus groups and informal interactions may include conversations and observations. For example, in the Learning Center, the sexuality brochures were placed on the bottom row of the slat wall along with other coping and side-effects materials. Patrons rarely asked for information on sexuality and the materials were not used. The sexuality pamphlets were moved to eye level, where they were taken regularly even though no one ever asks about sexuality. Informal patron feedback can be very informative for collection development and reader advisory; it can also serve to improve the patron experience and connection to the library when patrons see their suggestions or ideas implemented. The last, and most important, element for excellent service is staff engagement. Staff that are passionate, whether it is about materials, patrons, or even the monthly statistics, are critical to providing the highest level of service. A passionate and engaged staff using patron feedback for continuous improvement can create a library that provides the highest level of customer service and feels like a community to staff and patrons alike.

FUTURE DIRECTIONS

Going forward, the Learning Center staff expect to continue to improve technical skills and subject knowledge. Currently staff are trying to figure out how best to include both patient-facing e-books and mobile apps into the collection. Part of that puzzle is working toward making web-based and mobile resources accessible to patients in the real and virtual places they are already visiting. Most importantly, staff will continue to create and maintain relationships and alliances with colleagues throughout the greater institution who have similar aims. Those relationships have consistently been an incubator for new programs and services and allow the Learning Center to demonstrate its value to colleagues throughout the institution.

## 9

The Big Health Library Umbrella

*Our Mandate to Provide Information
for All Literacy Abilities*

Jackie Davis, *Consumer Health Library, Sharp HealthCare*

It does not take long on the job for new consumer health librarians to wonder if the printed information they give out to customers is actually going to be helpful to them. This chapter will describe the unfolding experience of the consumer health librarian at Sharp HealthCare in San Diego, California. When she began to see blank and stressed looks in the eyes of the patients and other customers at the Community Health Library, she knew that something was amiss in their approach to providing health information. That something turned out to be an awareness of health literacy and how best to level the information playing field for all patients. Developing this awareness required learning, experimenting, locating, and delivering accessible materials to a wider audience, which then gave consumers the opportunity to truly partner in their health care.

Information specialists enjoy customer contact, carefully ferreting out the "real" information request through the reference interview and, given that the subject matter is human health, being mindful and cautious about obtaining the highest-quality medical information. They can derive professional satisfaction in resolving a reference request and making referrals to appropriate professionals and organizations (Ham and Liebermann, 2012). Assuming that new librarians are proficient at finding credible and trustable health information, with their early enthusiasm to be supportive they might find it tempting to give too much information and overwhelm patrons at a vulnerable moment in their circumstance.

Additionally, and without realizing it, the information that is provided might be too difficult to read—for a variety of reasons. But how would the librarian know? There is research that correlates demographics such as education, race, financial resources, disability, and age with literacy levels, but it would be out of place in a reference interview to assume any of these risk factors or to ask direct and personal questions. It is not unusual for a patron who has just received a difficult diagnosis to be anxious or scared. In addition, the patron at the reference desk might be the caregiver who is as distraught and overwhelmed as the patient over the news. In these cases, the ability to hear medical information plummets, and patients/family members may not be able to take in one more fact, no matter what their reading level (NLM, 2012). The reality for the librarian is that he or she will not be able to tell if a person has a barrier to reading and understanding, for whatever reason, by simply looking at and listening to them. Librarians are charged to listen with great sensitivity to the information request and assume from the outset that every customer will have difficulties comprehending, digesting, and using the written material (AHRQ, 2015).

EVOLVING DEFINITIONS

There are multiple definitions and understandings of health literacy and these have evolved over time. Some definitions lay the responsibility on the patients to bring literacy skills to their health care. This characterization is illustrated by a widely used definition, the Patient Protection and Affordable Care Act of 2010, Title V. This Act defines health literacy as "the degree to which an individual has the capacity to obtain, communicate, process, and understand basic health information and services to make appropriate health decisions" (CDC, 2015).

An alternative, and more fitting, definition is the more inclusive statement from the Institute of Medicine. Health literacy is "an interaction between the skills of individuals and the demands of health systems . . . [and] occurs when the expectations, preferences, and skills of individuals seeking health information and services meet the expectations, preferences, and skills of the people providing health information and services" (Committee on Health Literacy, 2004: 2). There is a mutual responsibility of patients to educate themselves so they can advocate for their own health and clinical staff to support the patient in this effort by making the information accessible. In a perfect scenario, this could happen, but there is a lot of room for embedding these practices into medicine today.

Within the library setting, there is no similar and mutual imperative. Librarians do not assess language fluency, reading ability, or numeracy skills to determine if the patient can read the pamphlets, understand the information, and comply with the steps necessary for health. They certainly do not ask the education level of patients or any other demographic detail that might help sort through the appropriate printed options. In their role as information specialists, librarians do not have access to patient health records, and the encounter is often a one-time event. The reference interview offers the only information that the librarian can use both to find the information and to tailor that material for the specific request of the patron. Yet they have the responsibility to provide information that will support customers' needs and to help them become an empowered self-advocate in their health care.

As individuals begin their career working in health librarianship, a thought may occur that there is something missing, a question as to whether the printed information given—even quality and trustworthy information—is really helping the customer. These are well-placed concerns. In looking for the answer, in combination with the professional passion for providing good materials, consumer health librarians are in a unique position of bridging both the clinical need to have knowledgeable patients, and the patient's need to be able to make the best decisions for his or her health as a partner with his or her doctor. The difficulties the public might have regarding information access, due to *any* learning challenge, can serve to energize and encourage library professionals to learn more about the social influences that impact health literacy. In so doing, librarians can contribute to the needs of their particular clients as well as the broader conversation within the discipline.

Mascarenhas, Kesavan, and Bernacchi (2013) discuss the issue as one of information asymmetry, which "refers to a social situation where information is known to some, but not all, participants in the system." Public libraries have a long tradition of providing equal access to information and have supported literacy efforts for decades (ALA, 2015). The Medical Library Association sponsors a site to help translate "medspeak" and offers many online resources and links to support librarians wanting knowledge about and skills for providing patient education and health literacy (MLA, 2015).

This emphasis is not just part of the job. It is a call-to-action, a call for justice for patient learning parity despite demographic and/or emotional vulnerabilities. The National Network of Libraries of Medicine lists the many detrimental effects low health literacy has on patients. The acute medical crisis becomes chronic, requiring more medical visits, trips to emergency rooms, and hospitalizations—and added costs to the patient, insurance companies, hospitals, and government support systems (NNLM, 2013). The medical world is complex. A patient's very health can hang in the balance when trying to navigate the structure of the health care system. The challenges vary from finding a doctor who takes a particular insurance, to signing consent forms that are written in dense legalese or locating the potential adverse effects of a medication. In these situations, the health librarian has the ability to open doors of information for the patron.

THE FIELD—THEN AND NOW

The first entry in PubMed on the subject "health literacy" can be found in 1985, but the MeSH term was introduced in 2010 (NLM, 2015b). A recent search on the phrase indicates that professional research expanded considerably in the 1990s. There has been an intensive focus on health literacy in the ensuing years, and thus the understanding around these concepts has grown. An example of this evolving body of awareness is the assumption that the abilities to read and write were all that was necessary to be a literate adult. Reading is clearly a basic requirement, but numeracy—the ability to understand and use numerical information—is critical for maneuvering in a mathematical world. For patients, this ability is required for reading a prescription bottle and even for calendaring appointments.

In the present world of ubiquitous technological advances, literacy as understood to be reading words and knowing arithmetic, is merely the basic requirement for functioning well. Communication skills today include an ease with media literacy such as the ability to function on the computer, Internet, smartphone, and various social media. The complexity increases with the massive availability of information. It is also critical to be able to weed out quackery and opinion in the process of locating credible sources of information. The 2003 National Assessment of Adult Literacy survey identified three literacy measurements: prose literacy, which is the ability to search for written information and understand and use the data; document literacy, which includes being able to function well with maps, job applications, and labels; and quantitative literacy, which includes the various mathematical tasks that are used in everyday activities (White and Dillow, 2005). As shown in figure 9.1, the intricacies and nuances of being a literate member of modern society demand a sophisticated ability to maneuver the demands of the era.

To be a successful advocate for one's own health, or that of a loved one, the same literacy abilities, and some additional and critical skills, are a requirement. As stated earlier, the fields of literacy and health literacy have expanded as the experts have made strides in their research and testing protocols. Many initiatives have been undertaken and tools have been created to educate both patient and clinician abilities to communicate effectively.

Patients also must have the motivation to follow up with their doctor's recommendations. For instance, they have to be willing to eat a lower sodium diet and less carbohydrates and to exercise more. A health scare is not always enough to persuade those seeking medical care to make big changes in their

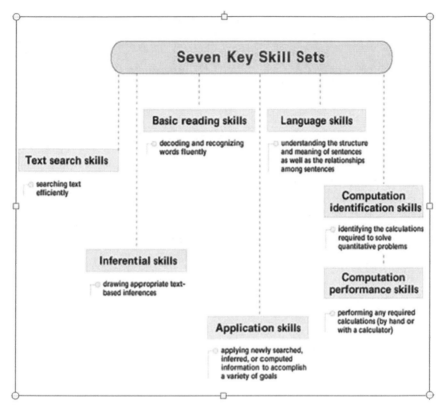

Figure 9.1.   Seven Key Skills Sets (Source: White, Sheida, and Sally Dillow. 2005. Key Concepts and Features of the 2003 National Assessment of Adult Literacy (NCES 2006-471). Washington, DC: National Center for Education Statistics, U.S. Department of Education, December. http://nces.ed.gov/NAAL/PDF/2006471.PDF)

routines. An additional and critical prerequisite is illustrated by the Patient Activation Measure, which looks at patient motivation, skills, and confidence for managing health and health care (Insignia Health, 2014). For example, Greene and colleagues showed that patient activation was more closely aligned with health outcomes such as chronic disease self-management, while health literacy was more closely related to the ability to use information in health-relevant decisions (AARP, 2005). It is at this juncture of patient education and patient motivation, Level 2, that consumer health librarians can impact a patient's experience and connection with his or her health care choices for action and for long-term compliance and maintenance of healthy behaviors (see figure 9.2).

Figure 9.2.   Patient Activation Measure Levels (© 2014 Insignia Health)

PRACTICES IN THE COMMUNITY HEALTH LIBRARY

Sharp HealthCare has invested in the Community Health Library in the Cushman Wellness Center, which is available to patients, families, and also the greater San Diego community. The library is located in the lobby of the Outpatient Pavilion, which is between the Sharp Memorial Hospital and the Mary Birch Hospital for Women and Newborns. There is a good deal of walk-in traffic from patients and families who are waiting for their loved ones who are having procedures. The Cancer Institute and Diabetes Education are the closest departments geographically, and services in the building include outpatient surgery, imaging, endoscopy procedures, and vision centers. The library resources include a vast collection of free pamphlets, books, videos, and CDs for check-out, and a quarterly newsletter that is sent out to approximately six hundred postal and e-mail addresses. In an effort to consistently reach out beyond the library walls, the staff attend local health and resource fairs and speak with community groups. Topics always include concepts like, "how best to speak with your doctor" and "where to find quality health information."

It did not take long for the current consumer health librarian to question whether handing someone a packet of information was going to guarantee that the patron would understand the content. Also in question was whether the information would be useful for patients' ongoing health concerns (speaking with their physician, making lifestyle changes, etc.). In fact, the initial, well-intended practice was to give too much information. It became clear that too much information might actually complicate the situation and overwhelm the customer. In these situations, the body language seemed to indicate frustration and confusion. Hardly any professional gratification could be found in these encounters! The patron often left unfulfilled and the librarian was frustrated with her inability to be helpful. It did not seem that the library was as supportive as it could be. Based on these experiences, the staff embarked upon a path both to understand the issues and then be in a position to respond to them. The assumption had to become that all consumers had challenges understanding and accessing medical information, and it was critical to provide the widest array of information options to the greatest number of patrons. The aim of this shift in services was to create an even playing field for those seeking knowledge and support for their health concerns.

PROFESSIONAL GROWTH OPPORTUNITIES

In a typical situation that might be faced by any new consumer health information professional, the Sharp librarian began her career with a general lack of professional knowledge, as well as the sense that there were no mentors to navigate these questions as they arose. It was clear that a concerted effort was needed for self-education. With a little research, it became evident that there are excellent resources easily available for librarians to grow professionally—and compassionately—in this field, and the additional good news is that there are many avenues and subject experts available for guidance. Ultimately, there would be many such reasons to enlist and join with others within the health organization, with local leaders, and even with librarians in the public library setting, all having the same determination and commitment to support patient education and self-advocacy. The initial online class identified was the Unified Health Communication, which has now changed its name to "Effective Communication Tools for Healthcare Professionals." It is a comprehensive course with five modules and is self-pacing. Content includes acquiring skills in order to

- acknowledge cultural diversity and deal sensitively with cultural differences that affect the way patients navigate the health care system,
- address low health literacy and bridge knowledge gaps that can prevent patients from adhering to prevention and treatment protocols, and
- accommodate low English proficiency and effectively use tools that don't rely on the written or spoken word (HRSA, 2015).

As an initial effort to apply these tools in the Sharp health library setting, consumer-oriented pamphlets, books, DVDs, and CDs were purchased in Spanish. There are many visitors to the library that either speak Spanish as a primary language or have family members that do, and there was a real need to provide trustable information to these patrons. The next step on the journey was learning how to determine the reading levels of the vast collection of pamphlets in the Community Health Library. The gold standard for health information on the web is MedlinePlus. There are no advertisements, thus the links are credible without concern of financial bias. Publications are available in over forty different languages. When researching information on Medline-Plus, the librarian frequently used the "Easy to Read" link. These materials seemed to span a range of reading levels. The website, under the "About" tab, indicates the variety of levels possible in the materials:

> MedlinePlus does not decide the literacy level of materials. The people who write the materials are the ones who decide if they are easy to read. In general, easy to read materials are usually written at a 5th to 8th grade reading level. The summaries on our health topic pages aim for a 5th to 8th grade reading level. (NLM, 2015a)

The National Assessment of Adult Literacy survey indicates that 43 percent of adults read at the below basic (grades 2–3) and basic levels (grades 4–5) (DCF, 2015). Using these numbers as a standard for evaluating easy-to-read health information, the majority of material in MedlinePlus that is accessible for lower reading skills is beyond the reach of many readers. As the librarian looked for pamphlets that aimed for a lower reading level, they were few and far between. It was common, however, to find materials that were developed for sixth-grade abilities. The caveat on the website made clear that while MedlinePlus was a great resource, it was important to view the language level and also have supplemental materials available.

Databases purchased by medical libraries for research by professional clinicians often have a patient education module that is included in the subscription price. Each were evaluated for reading level, which was often fifth or sixth grade (but also easy-to-find material in eighth grade), and for the number of pamphlets in other languages. Additionally, there are a number of for-profit companies that have developed pamphlets for consumers in a wide range of health topics. With a budget category designated specifically for pamphlets, these materials have been an excellent supplement to web resources. There is a particular sensitivity in these pamphlets to lifestyle graphics that reinforce the message as well as the need for white space. These characteristics of good consumer health information are helpful to consumers with lower literacy abilities, which makes the information easier to read for a larger portion of the consumer population.

The Consumer and Patient Health Information Section (CAPHIS) of the Medical Library Association offers many excellent courses toward obtaining the Consumer Health Information Specialization, most of which are easily available online. The librarian registered for the class, "Promoting Health Literacy through Easy-to-Read Materials." In addition to the information presented in the course, the instructor included a variety of websites that had easy-to-read materials for future reference.

The librarian spoke with everyone at the hospital who might already be aware of health literacy concerns. She expected that there would be local community groups working on this together in their different medical institutions. Through networking with Sharp staff, she was connected with the Community Health Improvement Partners (CHIP) Task Force on Health Literacy, who, in fact, had been gathering information on local and national resources and meeting regularly to discuss and plan for disseminating the findings. The Task Force, in collaboration with the San Diego Council on Literacy and many local leaders of health organizations and literacy programs, had developed a document titled, *When Words Get in the Way* (CHIP and San Diego Council on Literacy, 2009). This report is a superb education, as it outlines the broad issues and consequences of low health literacy in individual lives, both for the medical community and for the country. Examples include the stories of patients who cannot read prescription labels, and the document lists the numeracy skills required to follow directions, such as "take one pill in the morning and one at night." People with low health literacy often do not see their doctor regularly and have challenges with insurance coverage, making appointments, and calendaring correctly. In fact, many patients (of all reading abilities) walk out of their doctor's appointment without understanding what was said, and as a result, do not comply with "doctor's orders." People who struggle with grasping the scope of their health condition, obtaining office appointments, and following the directions of the health care provider, rather than using a primary care visit, go to the emergency room for immediate care and maybe hospitalization. Without solving the issues that get them there, conditions can become chronic, which may necessitate repeated hospitalizations. This cycle increases morbidity and mortality rates for patients. The financial burden for low health literacy is borne by the entire country.

The CHIP Task Force developed proposals that included the development of a website to house local resources as well as a plan for writing a curriculum specifically for adults reading at or below the third-grade level for introducing and reinforcing basic health concepts. Additionally, the Task Force prepared presentations for front- and back-office medical personnel, and committee members presented these talks to numerous local community clinics, professional associations, and students in vocational schools who worked in health settings. The Sharp health librarian took part in presenting to these audiences. One of the clearest tools included in these talks included the video from the American Medical Association that illustrates, with real patients and doctors, the "frustration and complications" associated with low health literacy (AMA, 2010). These Task Force presentations also contained information from The Agency for Healthcare, Research and Quality (AHRQ) Health Literacy Universal Precautions Toolkit (2015). This research affirms the need to use these tools with all patients, which then eliminates the need to assess the literacy levels. Furthermore, staff should not be in the position of deciding which patients require special services; instead they should assume that they will provide these literacy supports for everyone.

The Task Force also included role-playing scenarios that offered the attendees opportunities to both see and practice the techniques that support patient communication. The emphasis was on the "teach-back" technique with the responsibility on the provider for ensuring that all patients walk out of their appointment with a clear knowledge of what to do. This scenario does not focus on the patient's knowledge so much as it tests whether the provider communicated effectively.

When the Sharp health librarian presents to local groups on how best to advocate for themselves in the health care setting, she demonstrates an additional technique called the "self-initiated teach-back." In this scenario, the patient says, "Doctor, may I say back to you what I think I heard you say?" When role-playing this method, people feel empowered to take their share of responsibility for ensuring that communication with their provider is clear. In this way, both the clinicians are learning an oral approach to check the grasp of the patient, and the patient is also being given a tool that they can use to assure that they will walk out of their appointment with the accurate knowledge and understanding.

The Health Literacy Task Force has adopted both techniques in their presentations for health professionals, and these will be included in the updated report that is now being developed for publication in 2016. This report will have a more informed and broader understanding of the impact low literacy, and low health literacy, has on communities and society. It also shows more understanding of effective practices for all patients across literacy abilities.

The librarian also joined the very active and informative Health Literacy listserv, hosted by the Institute for Health Care Advancement (http://listserv. ihahealthliteracy.org/scripts/wa.exe?INDEX). The membership is international and includes people who have been working in the field for many years. The listserv is also a great place for those new to the discussion to learn from the best. The topics and discussions have informed and guided a number of initiatives in the Sharp library such as learning about the "Plain Language Thesaurus for Health Communications" (https://depts.washington.edu/respcare/public/info/Plain_Language_Thesaurus_for_Health_Communications.pdf) and the Plain Language Medical Dictionary (http://www.lib.umich.edu/taubman-health-sciences-library/plain-language-medical-dictionary).

The health library staff have been engaged in broad efforts to reach and teach people in many settings, in and out of the library itself, on how and where to find good quality health information on their own. There is a commitment to taking the library beyond the walls and out to the community, such as giving presentations to community groups associated with schools, senior centers, churches, and clubs. In these presentations, library staff share practical ideas about making the best of the time with their doctor during what is most often a very short appointment. When present at local health and resource fairs, staff also provide attendees with printed health information, pens, and bookmarks from MedlinePlus, and often a "give-away" with the contact information for the library. There are demonstrations to the public on using the MedlinePlus website and how best to find quality health and wellness information on the Internet. The goal is to teach people how to become better advocates in the medical institutions for their own health, and the anecdotal responses from attendees at these events have been positive. The library staff also inform people about the services available in the Community Health Library. It is open to the public, and it is free to borrow the books, videos, and CDs. Furthermore there are many ways for interested persons to request and obtain trustable health information, as the staff e-mail and send out links and also print articles and send them through the mail.

In previous years, Sharp Memorial nursing staff saw the need to address health literacy as a way to improve patient education, compliance, safety, and satisfaction across the hospital, and they created a Patient Education Council. This initiative was a response to the patient Hospital Consumer Assessment of Healthcare Providers and Systems (HCAHPS) scores that include a satisfaction domain on nursing communication, especially with regards to understanding the adverse effects of prescription medicine, as well as discharge instructions. The librarian contributed to the work of the committee by monitoring the Health Literacy Listserv and the results from other research sources such as PubMed, and continues to forward information to the committee chair and any other hospital departments that want to enhance their communication practices. The librarian attends unit staff meetings to demonstrate the databases with patient education modules. She focuses on the attributes of the modules to provide information at the fifth- to sixth-grade reading level and also in the number of languages available. Krames Staywell, just one of many commercial health handout providers, can be personalized, and additional instructions may be typed into the material. Patient Education Reference Center aims to write materials for the third- through seventh-grade levels and, like Krames, to supply many subjects in Spanish. Each of these companies puts a value on easy reading levels with illustrations that match the message. These resources are invaluable tools for staff and physicians as they prepare patients for discharge.

The library department also implemented a Health Information Ambassador program (Davis, 2013). Specially chosen and trained volunteers make rounds to patient rooms in the hospital and ask patients and families if they would like to have any further information about their health or diagnosis. The volunteers bring the requests back to the librarian, who obtains the printed material, and the volunteer returns it to the patient. There are multiple benefits for the patient with this program. Information can be printed in the easiest-to-read levels and in the requested language. The volunteer also has the extra time to spend with the patient. It is this extra time that is of great value to both the patient and the volunteer. During the encounter, patients often feel cared about, and the delivery of a packet of information the individual requests highlights the context of this caring relationship. The materials are more supportive for the patient within this brief but real connection. The volunteer also leaves the librarian's card with the invitation to call or e-mail for further information post-discharge. These efforts align with clinical staff initiatives and support not only patient education, but patient activation/ motivation through warm, human interaction.

APPLYING THE PRINCIPLES IN AN EVIDENCE-BASED PROJECT

In 2015, the Sharp health librarian was invited to become a fellow in an Evidence-Based Project Institute (EBPI) Consortium for Nursing Excellence in San Diego. The project assigned to the team was health literacy and, although the institute is focused on nursing research, it was believed that with the librarian's interest and knowledge about health literacy and experience with medical research she would be a good member of the team.

While there is much professional literature discussing the "teach back" tool, which is implemented at the end of the hospital stay, this project concentrated on the front-end communication regarding both the assessment of abilities to understand the situation that brought the patient to the hospital and, in general, whether the patient will be able to understand written information. In addition, patient satisfaction with nurse communication was critical for measuring the success of the project.

The literature about assessment looks at a variety of tools that measure reading levels. There is research that shows patient discomfort with many of the ways their literacy level is evaluated and that points to the lack of dignity these tools afford the patient (Patel et al., 2011). There is also research that indicates patient acceptance and support for assessments, especially when patients understand how their answers will impact their care (VanGeest, Welch, and Weiner, 2010). Even with these differing research results, most of the tools used are only appropriate for the primary care setting.

The librarian's role on the team was primarily to explore the professional and expert research to support the project and to help to create a new practice for front-end assessment on behalf of a unit that had low HCAHPS scores in the nurse communication domain. The research has determined that it is critical for clinical staff to assess individual abilities, using sensitive protocols, in order to provide the most appropriate patient education. The tools have evolved over the years and include evaluating reading and math skills, considering specific demographics and gauging language skills. Beyond these objective measures that help the clinician offer effective printed materials, there is the concept of the clinician taking the lead in going beyond simply handing the patient printed information and calling it "patient education." People absorb information best in the context of a relationship, and providers can "engage the patient" within this caring context. This sense of connection impacts post-appointment compliance (CFAH, 2010). The research also underscored the value of offering a warm welcome to customers in the consumer health library setting (Spatz, 2008). An intentional and caring atmosphere allows customers to feel safe to ask for the information that they need and to receive the materials within a context of engagement as well as being educational. This was a goal of the project—to implement a technique that the unit staff could use for all patients and to learn if this was an effective opening for both nurse and patient interaction.

After the librarian gathered the research identifying the best practices for assessing the health literacy level of patients, the evidence-based project team initiated a unique protocol that would be used with every new patient on the Progressive Care Unit. The RN would ask the patient, "What do you know about (your health condition)?" This helps the RN identify the skills and knowledge of the patients—their health literacy—so the staff would know what to teach. The second question is, "What would you like to know about (your health condition)?" This additional question is meant to engage and motivate patients to partner in their own health care. Performed consistently, the project hoped to show that the verbal questions were appropriate for *every* patient and would open the lines of caring, effective communication with *every* patient from the outset. The measure of effect would be patient satisfaction HCAHPS scores within the nurse communication domain, as shown by an increase in the HCAHPS scores. An additional data point would be the pre- and post-survey of staff knowledge of health literacy, thus identifying any additional staff education needs and practices.

The project and protocol were presented at the monthly Unit Practice Council meeting for questions and input. Subsequently, the librarian gave the PowerPoint presentation at the full staff meeting, introducing foundational information about health literacy, the value of patient education, and the project goal of activating patient engagement, which would motivate investment in his or her own healing. The nurse team member who worked on that particular unit continued the presentation of the project with specifics for implementation, the time frames for staff surveys, and the peer reward system that was implemented. The completed statistics will be gathered at the end of the year, and a report will be prepared for the institute.

BEST PRACTICES AND ONGOING EFFORTS

This chapter, and log of a personal journey, illustrates many instances where professional education has improved the understanding of health literacy and how best to address the many needs of all consumers of health information. With the ethical and economical stakes of health care and individual well-being so high, it is critical to broaden professional core competencies to include health literacy skills.

Collaboration

The lesson most clearly learned was the value of speaking with everyone in the hospital, and in the community, in order to find the knowledgeable people, resources, and institutions working in this arena. Both the Sharp Patient Education Committee and the San Diego Task Force on Health Literacy strongly shaped the services offered to customers, and ultimately, the librarian has since been instrumental in supporting the health literacy initiatives at Sharp HealthCare and community programs.

Professional Education

The online courses offered through the Medical Library Association, as well as other organizations, have clarified issues and compelled action. It was through these classes that the librarian was referred to the work at the National Network of Libraries of Medicine (NNLM, 2013). The section, "Role of the Consumer Health Librarian" listed practical steps to take for both self-education and action. The Health Literacy Listserv remains an invaluable tool to learn about cutting-edge research, practices, and conferences exploring the issues and striving toward solutions. It is a rich moment in medicine for librarians to improve their ability to be patient information advocates and to link the health library with other initiatives moving in this direction.

Locating Free Resources

In the effort to seek out sources for pamphlets with attention to lower reading levels, the librarian found the patient education modules often included in the subscription's medical information databases. In addition to MedlinePlus, there are multiple for-profit companies that provide handouts for patients with a dedicated focus on accessibility. These vendors were very helpful in unpacking readability levels and addressing how their products reinforce good health behaviors in their materials. The National Institutes of Health also sponsor many websites, and anyone may order pamphlets or print from the links.

CONCLUSION AND MANDATE

The present-day need for patients to advocate successfully, and partner intelligently, in their health care is requiring additional skill sets for consumer health librarians. To this end, it is vital to bring health literacy concerns front and center to meet the educational needs of all customers: patients, caregivers, and community members. A large disparity still exists in the accessibility of quality health information in many current health care venues. There is much work and research to do. Fortunately, evidence-based inquiries and project development are in place to improve ways to support patient-provider communication. There is more clinical interest in the topic at this moment in medical history. Consumer health libraries are positioned to include services and resources to support both professional and lay concerns and to promote hospital-wide attention to health literacy issues and resources for the widest audience and variety of information needs. In this era of widespread awareness, exploration, and rich discussion with regards to health literacy, the library profession is poised to address this mandate to provide quality information to every customer at an accessible literacy level for all patients, to expand knowledge of the health literacy field, and to contribute to the solutions. It is incumbent upon our libraries to persevere in efforts to provide useful information and to partner with other professionals and community members to create new solutions for health literacy challenges.

REFERENCES

AARP (American Association of Retired Persons). 2005. "How Much Do Health Literacy and Patient Activation Contribute to Older Adults' Abilities to Manage Their Health." June. http://assets.aarp.org/rgcenter/health/2005_05_literacy.pdf.

AHRQ (Agency for Healthcare Research and Quality). 2015. *AHRQ Health Literacy Universal Precautions Toolkit.* 2nd ed. February. http://www.ahrq.gov/professionals/quality-patient-safety/qulity-resources/tools/literacy-toolkit/index.html.

ALA (American Library Association). 2015. "American Library Association—Leading the Way for Literacy." Last updated 2015. http://www.ala.org/news/mediapress center/factsheets/leadingwayliteracy.

AMA (American Medical Association). 2010. "Health Literacy and Patient Safety: Help Patients Understand." August 27. https://www.youtube.com/watch?v=cGtTZ_vxjyA.

CDC (Centers for Disease Control and Prevention). 2015. "Learn about Health Literacy." Last updated April 10. http://www.cdc.gov/healthliteracy/Learn/index.html.

CFAH (Center for Advancing Health). 2010. "Snapshot of People's Engagement in Their Health Care." 2010. http://www.cfah.org/file/CFAH_Snapshot_Summary_2010.pdf.

CHIP (Community Health Improvement Partners) and San Diego Council on Literacy. 2009. *When Words Get in the Way: A Collaborative Plan to Address Health Literacy in San Diego County.* http://www.healthliteracysd.org/media/92865/wwgitw_healthliteracyreport_final.pdf.

Committee on Health Literacy. 2004. *Health Literacy: A Prescription to End Confusion.* Washington, DC: National Academies Press.

Davis, Jackie. 2013. "Health Information Ambassador Program for Patient Education: A Best Practice for Bringing the Consumer Health Library to the Patient." *Journal of Consumer Health on the Internet* 17, no. 1 (February): 25–34.

DCF (Wisconsin Department of Children and Families). 2015. "Educational Functioning Level Descriptors for PS45 Literacy and Numeracy Gains Standard." http://dcf.wisconsin.gov/w2/pdf/descriptors_table.pdf.

Ham, Kelli, and Jana Liebermann. 2012. "The Consumer Health Reference Interview and Ethical Issues." NNLM. Last updated July 9. https://nnlm.gov/outreach/consumer/ethics.html.

HRSA (Health Resources and Services Administration). 2015. "Health Literacy." May. http://www.hrsa.gov/publichealth/healthliteracy/.

Insignia Health. 2014. "Patient Activation Measure." InsigniaHealth.com. http://www.insigniahealth.com/solutions/patient-activation-measure/.

Mascarenhas, Oswald A., Ram Kesavan, and Michael D. Bernacchi. 2013. "On Reducing Information Asymmetry in U.S. Health Care." *Health Marketing Quarterly* 30: 379–98.

MLA (Medical Library Association). 2015. "Health Information Literacy." June. https//www.mlanet.org/resources/healthlit/index.html.

NLM (National Library of Medicine). 2012. "The Consumer Health Reference Interview and Ethical Issues." National Network of Libraries of Medicine. https://nnlm.gov/outreach/consumer/ethics.html.

NLM (National Library of Medicine). 2015a. "Easy-to-Read." Last updated August 3. http://www.nlm.nih.gov/medlineplus/faq/easytoread.html.

NLM (National Library of Medicine). 2015b. "MeSH. Health Literacy." NCBI. National Library of Medicine. Last updated June 16. http://www.ncbi.nlm.nih.gov/mesh/68057220.

NNLM (National Network of Libraries of Medicine). 2013. "Health Literacy." NLM (National Library of Medicine). Last updated June. http://nnlm.gov/outreach/consumer/hlthlit.html.

Patel, Pragnesh J., Joel Steinberg, Rovena Goveas, et al. 2011. "Testing the Utility of the Newest Vital Sign (NVS) Health Literacy Assessment Tool in Older African-American Patients." *Patient Education and Counseling* 85, no. 3 (March): 505–7.

Spatz, Michele. 2008. *Answering Consumer Health Questions: The Medical Library Association Guide for Reference Librarians.* New York: Neal-Schuman Publishers.

VanGeest, J. B., V. L. Welch, and S. J. Weiner. 2010. "Patients' Perceptions of Screening for Health Literacy: Reactions to the Newest Vital Sign." *Journal of Health Communication: International Perspectives* 15, no. 4: 402–12.

White, Sheida, and Sally Dillow. 2005. *Key Concepts and Features of the 2003 National Assessment of Adult Literacy.* (NCES 2006-471). Washington, DC: National Center for Education Statistics, U.S. Department of Education, December. http://nces.ed.gov/NAAL/PDF/2006471.PDF.

Index

Page references for figures and tables are italicized

Academy of Health Information Professionals (AHIP), 29
accessibility, 5, 10–11
advisory committees, 38–39, 42, 44
American Library Association: Code of Ethics of the American Library Association, 62–63; Library Bill of Rights, 61–62
Asian language materials, 59
assessment. *See* evaluation

Baystate Health, Consumer Health Library, 88–101; collaboration, 89–100; data-driven outreach, 92–99; Data-Driven Playbook, 96–99; Data-Driven Playbook Logic Model, *97*; evaluation, 94–96; lessons learned, 99; needs assessment, 94–96; physical space, 89; public services, 89
Baystate Health, Health Sciences Library, 88–89; mission statement, *88*
best practices, 15–16, *31–32*, 58, 103–109, 116–117, 131–132, 146–147;

evaluation criteria, *3*; *See also* lessons learned
book fairs, 60–61
bookmobile, 92–94, *93*
Brigham and Women's Faulkner Hospital Patient/Family Resource Center (P/FRC), 1–18; accessibility, 5–6, 9–13; best practices, 3, 15–16; budgeting/funding, 11–12; collaboration, 9–11; collection development, 3–6; evaluation, 13–14; future, 15; goals and objectives, 2; library staff, 7–8, 12; mission statement, 2; patient services, 5–6, 9–13; promotion, *7*; public services, 5–6, 9–13; resources, services, and programs, 3–7; volunteers, 8–9, 12; website resources, 5
budgeting/funding, 11–12, 39–41, 47, 68–69, 120

Cancer Consumer Health Library. *See* MD Anderson Cancer Center Learning Center

CAPHIS. *See* Medical Library
Association: Consumer and
Patient Health Information Section
(CAPHIS)
Chicopee Public Library, 89–100;
collaboration, 89–100; CPL
Bookmobile, 92–94, *93*; Data-
Driven Playbook, 96–99; Data-
Driven Playbook Logic Model,
97; evaluation, 94–96; data-driven
outreach, 92–99; lessons learned,
99; mission statement, *90*; needs
assessment, 94–96; public services,
90–91, 95–96
circulation services, 125
Code of Ethics for Health Sciences
Librarianship, 63–65
Code of Ethics of the American Library
Association, 62–63
collaboration, 9–11, 36–39, 57–58,
69–70, 89–100, 110, 146
collaborative outreach, 87–101
collection development, 3–6, 28,
41–42, 52–54, 110–111, 126–128;
evaluation, *3*
community outreach. *See* outreach
community partnerships. *See*
collaboration
computer/information literacy, 106–107
construction planning, 26–30
Consumer and Patient Health
Information Section (CAPHIS).
See Medical Library Association,
Consumer and Patient Health
Information Section (CAPHIS)
Consumer Health Information
Specialization (CHIS). *See* Medical
Library Association: Consumer and
Patient Health Information Section
(CAPHIS)
customer service. *See* public services

data collection, 121–122
Data-Driven Playbook, 96–99
Data-Driven Playbook Logic Model, *97*

dental health education for preschoolers,
76; stories for, 84–85
Department of Veterans Affairs Library
Network. *See* Veterans Affairs
Library Network (VALNET)
Diabetes Wellness Clinics, 104–105

eBenefits (VA), 107
ethical concerns. *See* legal/ethical
concerns
evaluation, 13–14, 21–22, 23–24, 30–
32, 45–47, 52, 94–96, 131
evidence-based CHI project, 144–146
exercise education for preschoolers,
72–73; stories for, 82

Farsi/Persian language materials, 59
floor plan, *27*
focus groups, 36–37
foreign language resources, 59–61
free resources, 147
French language materials, 59
funding. *See* budgeting/funding

Go Local. *See* National Library of
Medicine, Go Local program
goals and objectives, *2*, 67–68

hand hygiene education for
preschoolers, 74–75; stories for, 83
Health InfoNet of Alabama, 35–49;
Advisory Committee, 38–39, 42;
budgeting/funding, 39–41, 47;
collaboration, 38–39; collection
development, 41–42; community
outreach, 43–44, 48; evaluation, 45–
47; Go Local, 40–41; history, 35–38;
lessons learned, 47–48; library staff,
47; marketing, 42; mission statement,
37–38; needs assessment, 36–38;
organization, 38–39, 47; post-Go
Local, 44–45; staff training, 39
health literacy, 133–149; defined,
134–136; history, 136–137; mandate
for health libraries, 147; Patient

Activation Measure, 137, *138*; Seven Key Skills Sets, *137*

heart health education for preschoolers, 73–74; stores for, 83–84

Hospital Consumer Assessment of Healthcare Providers and Systems (HCAHPS) scores, 143–144

information prescriptions, 104

inpatient delivery services, 125

Kaiser-Permanente Medical Center (Oakland, CA), 57–58

Knox County Public Library, 20

legal/ethical concerns, 55

lessons learned, 47–48, 78–79, 99; *See also* best practices

Library Bill of Rights, 61–62

library construction, 26–30; floor plan, *27*

library staff, 7–8, 12, 29, 47, 121, 143; training, 39, 55–56

Lister Hill Library of the Health Sciences. *See* Health InfoNet of Alabama

Louis Stokes Cleveland VA Medical Center: PERC Packs, 112–116

LSU Health Shreveport Health Sciences Library, community partnership, 67–86; goals and objectives, 67–68

marketing, 42, 128–129; *See also* outreach; promotion/publicity

MD Anderson Cancer Center Learning Center, 119–132; best practices, 131–132; budgeting/funding, 130; circulation services, 125; collection development, 126–128; customer service, 123–124; data collection, 121–122; evaluation, 131; facilities, 120; history, 119–120; inpatient delivery services, 125; library staff, 121; outreach/marketing, 128–129; pathfinders, 129–130;

patient feedback, 123; podcasts, 130–131; public computers, 126; public services, 123–127; QR codes, 128; reference services, 124–125; technology assistance, 126; web statistics form, *122*

Medical Library Association: Academy of Health Information Professionals (AHIP), 29; Code of Ethics for Health Sciences Librarianship, 63–65; Consumer and Patient Health Information Section (CAPHIS), 56, 140–141; Consumer Health Information Specialization (CHIS), 29, 56, 140–141; Definition of health literacy, 135

McdlincPlus. *See* National Library of Medicine: MedlinePlus

mission statement, 2, 37–38, *88*, *90*

My HealtheVet, 107, 109

National Library of Medicine: Go Local program, 40–41, 44–45; MedlinePlus, 5, 11, 43, 53, 107, 140; training, 55–56

National Network of Libraries of Medicine, 43, 88; definition of health literacy, 135; training, 56, 146

National Network of Libraries of Medicine/New England Region (NN/LM NER), 11, 90

National Network of Libraries of Medicine South Central Region (NN/LM SCR), 68–69

National Network of Libraries of Medicine, Southeastern Atlantic (NNLM/SE/A) Region, 23, 24, 38, 39

NCLIS Award, 21

needs assessment, 22–23, 36–38, 94–06

nutrition education for preschoolers, 71–72; stories for, 80–82

Oakland Public Library (CA), 57–58

organization, 38–39, 47

Orlando Public Library, 110
Orlando VA Medical Center Library,
109–112; collection development,
110–111; needs assessment,
110; partnership with Orlando
Public Library, 110; public access
computers, 109–110; public services,
110–112; recreational reading
collection, 110
outpatient clinics, 104–105
outreach, 22–23, 24–25, 43–44, 48, 56–
57, 128–129; data-driven, 92–99; *See
also* marketing; promotion/publicity

partnerships. *See* collaboration
pathfinders, 129–130
Patient Activation Measure, 137, *138*
patient education, 30, 105
patient feedback, 123
patient services, 5–6, 9–13, 123–127,
129
PERC Packs, 112–116; Clinician Cover
Sheet, *113*; evolution/expansion,
114–116; Patient Cover Sheet, *113*
Perkins Institute Braille and Talking
Book Library, 10–11
physical space, 25–28, 88–89, 120
Planetree Model, 108–109
podcasts, 130–131
preschoolers, wellness for: budgeting/
funding, 68–69; collaboration,
69–70; goals and objectives, 67–68;
lessons learned, 78–79; promotion/
publicity, 76–77; recommended
stories, 80–85; rewards, 77–78;
stories and activities, 70–76; web
portal, 69
Preston Medical Library and Health
Information Center (CHIS), 19–34;
best practices, *31–32*; collection
development, 28; construction
planning, 26–30; evaluation, 21–22,
23–24, 30–32; floor plan, *27*; history,
19–20; library staff, 29; NCLIS

Award, 21; needs assessment, 22–23;
outreach, 22–23, 24–25; patient
education, 30; physical space, 26–28;
public access computers, 28; public
services, 29–30; Simple Plan, 24–25;
surveys, 21–22, 30–31
professional education, 146–147
professional growth opportunities,
139–144
promotion/publicity, *7*, 76–77; *See also*
marketing; outreach
public access computers, 28, 89, 90,
107, 109–110, 126
public libraries, consumer health
information services in: best
practices, 58; Code of Ethics for
Health Sciences Librarianship,
63–65; Code of Ethics of the
American Library Association, 62–
63; collaboration, 57–58; collection
development, 52–54; community
assessment, 52; foreign language
resources, 59–61; legal/ethical
concerns, 55; Library Bill of Rights,
61–62; outreach, 56–57; reference
interview, 54–55; role of public
library, 51; staff training, 55–56
Public Library Association, 55
public services, 5–6, 9–13, 29–30, 89,
90–91, 95–96, 110–112, 123–127

QR codes, 128

recreational reading collections, 108,
110
reference interview, 54–55
reference services, 124–125
Russian language materials, 60

Sci-Port (Louisiana's Science Center),
70, 75, 77
Seven Key Skills Sets, *137*
Sharp HealthCare (San Diego, CA):
Community Health Improvement

Partners (CHIP) Task Force, 141–142; Community Health Library, 138–139; Evidence-Based Project Institute (EBPI) Consortium, 144–146; Health Information Ambassador Program, 144; Health Literacy listserv, 142–143; Health Literacy Task Force, 142; Hospital Consumer Assessment of Healthcare Providers and Systems (HCAHPS) scores, 143–144

Sharp HealthCare (San Diego, CA) Consumer Health Library, 133–149; best practices, 146–147; collaboration, 146; evidence-based project, 144–146; library staff, 143; professional education, 146–147; professional growth opportunities, 139–144; volunteers, 144

Shreve Memorial Library, 69–76

Simple Plan, 24–25

sleep habits education for preschoolers, 76; stories for, 84

social networking support, 107

Spanish language materials, 55, 60, 105, 139–140

staff. *See* library staff

stories for preschoolers, 70–76, 80–85

Stroke Patient Book Club, 105–106

sun safety education for preschoolers, 75

surveys, 21–22, 30–31, 36, 46; *See also* evaluation

technology assistance, 126

training. *See* library staff, training

University of Alabama Lister Hill Library. *See* Health InfoNet of Alabama

University of Tennessee Medical Center. *See* Preston Medical Library and Health Information Center

utilization. *See* evaluation

VALNET. *See* Veterans Affairs Library Network (VALNET)

Veterans Affairs Library Network (VALNET), 103–117; best practices in consumer health, 103–109; best practices in patient-centered care, 116–117; computer/information literacy, 106–107; Diabetes Wellness Clinics, 106–107; information prescriptions, 104; Louis Stokes Cleveland VA Medical Center, 112–116; My HealtheVet, 107, 109; Orlando VA Medical Center Library, 109–112; outpatient clinics, 104–105; patient education, 105; PERC Packs, 112–116; Planetree Model, 108–109; public access computers, 107, 109–110; recreational reading collections, 108, 110; social networking support, 107; Spanish outreach, 105; Stroke Patient Book Club, 105–106; ward carts, 108

volunteers, 8–9, 12, 144

ward carts, 108

web portal, 69

web statistics form, *122*

website resources, 5, 61

About the Editor and the Contributors

Laurie A. Barnett, MA (University of South Florida) is chief of library service at James A. Haley VA Veterans' Hospital (JAHVH) in Tampa, Florida. In 2002 the Federal Library and Information Center Committee (FLICC) named the JAHVH Library the "Best Federal Library/Information Center of the Year." JAHVH has three libraries; the medical library and a separate patient library are both in the main hospital, and a new Patient Education Resource Center is located in the Primary Care Annex.

Barbara M. Bibel received a BA in French from UCLA, an MA in Romance Languages from Johns Hopkins University, and an MLS from the University of California, Berkeley. She has Level-II accreditation as a Consumer Health Information Specialist from the Medical Library Association. She recently retired from her position as a reference librarian/consumer health information specialist at the Oakland Public Library in California.

Elizabeth Brackeen has a master's of science in information science from the University of North Texas. She has been a senior librarian in the Learning Center at MD Anderson Cancer Center since 2004. Prior to working in cancer consumer health, she was a library manager for Harris County Public Libraries and project manager for Ovid Technologies. Elizabeth is currently working on her doctorate in educational technology from the University of Houston, College of Education. Her research interest is online patient education.

Ellen Brassil, MSLS, MAT, DM/AHIP, is director of the Baystate Health Sciences Library in Springfield, Massachusetts. She has taught CE Courses and has been active in health sciences libraries at the regional and national level, and has published many book chapters, articles, and book reviews. She has served on the editorial board for the *Journal of the Medical Library Association* and as book review editor for the *Journal of Electronic Resources in Medical Libraries* and for *Medical Reference Services Quarterly*. Ellen has taught information courses to health sciences students and professionals at all levels, holds an MSLS from Simmons College, and earned a master's degree in teaching from Sacred Heart University. She has served on her town's Advisory Commission for Persons with Disabilities and was elected to her town's Board of Education three times.

Cornelia E. Camerer, MLS (University of Missouri) holds the position of chief of library services for the North Florida/South Georgia Veterans Health System in Gainesville, Florida. In her previous position she worked as medical librarian for Landstuhl Regional Medical Center (LRMC) and as the consultant to the Europe Regional Medical Command (ERMC). Under her stewardship, LRMC was named the 2007 "Best Federal Library/Information Center of the Year."

Teresa R. Coady, MLS (Emporia State University) is the library manager for the Orlando VA Medical Center in Orlando, Florida. Teresa has developed innovative programs to support improvement of veterans' health and library programs to support job training for Orlando veterans.

Jackie Davis is the consumer health librarian for Sharp HealthCare in San Diego. She has had the opportunity to work in many different library settings and has enjoyed the work in each of them. She has a particular interest in health literacy as well as social justice. Combining both of these passions has informed and guided her work in the library and the community. In 2013 Jackie received the Consumer Health Librarian Award from the Consumer and Patient Health Section of the Medical Library Association. She has published elsewhere on projects and programs implemented at Sharp. Additionally, she is a passionate fan of cat videos.

Martha F. Earl, MSLS, AHIP, serves as assistant director/associate professor at the University of Tennessee Medical Center, Health Information Center/Preston Medical Library, in Knoxville, where she has worked since 1997. She received her BS and her MSLS from the University of Tennessee. Previously she helped people to find the answers at both Meharry Medical College and East Tennessee State University College of Medicine Libraries. Martha has also contributed in a variety of leadership roles in the Medical Library

Association and her state associations, including career-long involvement in the Tennessee Library Association. Her outreach activities demonstrate the value of partnerships. She is a 2011–2012 NLM/AAHSL leadership fellow.

Anne Gancarz, MSLIS, is the community services librarian at the Chicopee Public Library in Chicopee, Massachusetts. Prior to working in libraries, Ms. Gancarz lived in New York City where she was a pre-doctoral fellow in the Department of Psychiatry and Behavioral Sciences at Memorial Sloan Kettering Cancer Center and worked as a research assistant for various projects on the psychology of health. Ms. Gancarz received her degree from Simmons College in 2010.

Diane K. Kromke, MLS (Kent State University) is the patient health education librarian in the Patient Education Resource Center at the Louis Stokes Cleveland VA Medical Center in Cleveland, Ohio. She was awarded the Medical Library Association's Specialization in Consumer Health Information in 2014.

Kelsey Leonard, MSIS, AHIP, is the health information services librarian at the Health Information Center and Preston Medical Library as well as an assistant professor at the University of Tennessee College of Medicine at the Knoxville campus, located at the University of Tennessee Medical Center. Kelsey received her master's in information science from the University of Tennessee and her bachelor of arts from the University of Mary Washington. Her research interests include working with patients and their family members to find health information, health literacy, and collection development.

Margot Malachowski, MLS, AHIP, is the community outreach librarian at the Baystate Health Sciences Library in Springfield, Massachusetts. She has written on CHI outreach for *Computers in Libraries, Journal of Consumer Health on the Internet,* and *Journal of Hospital Librarianship*. Ms. Malachowski currently serves on the executive board for the Massachusetts Library System and is the healthy communities leader for the National Network of Libraries of Medicine—New England Region. She holds a master of library science from Syracuse University and earned a Level II in the Medical Library Association's Consumer Health Information Specialist Program.

Cara Marcus, MSLIS, AHIP, was director of library services for Brigham and Women's Faulkner Hospital from 2008–2015. A graduate of the Simmons College Graduate School of Library and Information Science, Marcus has founded collections for Brigham and Women's Hospital's Kessler Library and the Harvard University Kennedy School of Government Health Care Delivery Policy

Program. She has served as president of the Massachusetts Health Sciences Library Network and as chair of the MLA CAPHIS managing a CHIS review committee. Her publications include books, book chapters, and journal articles on topics including health literacy, archives and history of medicine, health care delivery, and consumer health information services.

Sandy Oelschlegel, MLIS AHIP, is the director of the Health Information Center and Preston Medical Library and an associate professor in the University of Tennessee College of Medicine at the Knoxville campus, which is located at the University of Tennessee Medical Center. She is a graduate of the University of Rhode Island Graduate School of Library and Information Science. Her research is focused on information needs and patterns in an academic medical center, health information literacy, and evaluation of medical library services and resources.

Kay Hogan Smith, MLS, MPH, CHES, is professor and chair of Public/Community Health Services at the University of Alabama at Birmingham Lister Hill Library of the Health Sciences, where she has worked for over twenty years. Kay has directed the Health InfoNet of Alabama project from its beginning in 1999. She received her MLS from the University of Alabama in 1985 and her MPH from the University of Alabama at Birmingham in 2012. Kay is a certified health educator, and her research interest is focused on health literacy issues.

Priscilla L. Stephenson, MSLS, MSEd, AHIP (University of Kentucky and Northern Illinois University) is chief of library services at the Crescenz VA Medical Center in Philadelphia, Pennsylvania. She is a past chair of both the Federal Libraries Section and the Hospital Libraries Section of MLA and coeditor of columns in the *Journal of Consumer Health Information* and *Medical Reference Services Quarterly*.

Donna F. Timm is currently the head of User Education at the LSU Health Shreveport Health Sciences Library and has held that position since 2003. She coordinates the library's educational and outreach programs, offering database searching and consumer-health training classes and events. Her degrees are as follows: AA in paralegal studies, Dover College, Dover, Delaware, 1987; BA in English, Lenoir Rhyne University, Hickory, North Carolina, 1973; and MLS, University of North Carolina at Greensboro, 1978.

M. Sandra Wood, MLS, MBA, FMLA, is librarian emerita, Penn State University Libraries, and a fellow of the Medical Library Association. Ms.

Wood is founding and current editor of *Medical Reference Services Quarterly* (in its thirty-fifth volume) and was founding editor of *Journal of Consumer Health on the Internet* (formerly *Health Care on the Internet*), which she edited for fifteen years. She was a librarian for over thirty-five years at the George T. Harrell Library, Milton S. Hershey Medical Center, Pennsylvania State University, specializing in reference, education, and database services. Ms. Wood has written or edited more than twelve books, including *Health Sciences Librarianship* (Rowman & Littlefield Publishers, 2014).

Deidra Woodson has been the metadata and digitization librarian at the LSU Health Shreveport Health Sciences Library since September 2008. Although her primary responsibilities include cataloging and digitization of the archives, she has also been actively involved in consumer health education within the local community and has helped to establish a successful children's health program. She is a certified and licensed Medical Technologist and holds master's degrees in both library science and English.